The Real-Time Enterprise

Other Books from Meghan-Kiffer Press

Business Process Management: The Third Wave
Howard Smith and Peter Fingar

Business Process Management: A Rigorous Approach
Martyn Ould, Co-published with the British Computer Society

IT Doesn't Matter—Business Processes Do
Howard Smith and Peter Fingar

Business Process Management: A Practical Guide
Rashid N. Khan

Business Process Management is a Team Sport:
Play it to Win!
Andrew Spanyi

The Death of 'e' and the Birth of the
Real New Economy
Peter Fingar and Ronald Aronica

Enterprise E-Commerce
Peter Fingar, Harsha Kumar and Tarun Sharma

Meghan-Kiffer Press
Tampa, Florida, USA
www.mkpress.com
Advanced Business-Technology Books for Competitive Advantage

The Real-Time Enterprise

Competing on Time Using the Revolutionary Business SEx Machine

Peter Fingar
Joseph Bellini

Meghan-Kiffer Press
Tampa, Florida, USA, www.mkpress.com
Advanced Business-Technology Books for Competitive Advantage

Publisher's Cataloging-in-Publication Data

Fingar, Peter.

The Real-Time Enterprise : Competing on Time Using the Revolutionary Business SEx Machine / Peter Fingar, Joseph Bellini, - 1st ed.

p. cm.

Includes bibliographic references, appendices and index.

ISBN 0-929652-30-4 (cloth : alk. paper)

1. Management 2. Technological innovation. 3. Strategic planning. 4. Management information systems. 5. Information technology. 6. Information resources management. 7. Organizational change. I. Fingar, Peter. II. Bellini, Joseph,. III. Title.

HF58.8..F464 2004   LC Control# 2002106052
658.8'00285-dc21   CIP

Published by Meghan-Kiffer Press
310 East Fern Street ❑ Suite G
Tampa, FL 33604 USA

Any product mentioned in this book may be a trademark of its company.

Cover Photo: NASA.

Cover Quotes: www.brainyquote.com

Meghan-Kiffer Press
Tampa, Florida, USA
Publishers of Advanced Business-Technology Books for Competitive Advantage
Printed in the United States of America.   SAN 249-7980
MK Printing 10 9 8 7 6 5 4 3 2 1

Dedicated to Alan Greenspan
for recognizing and articulating the competitive advantages
of the real-time enterprise.

"Doubtless, the substantial improvement in access of business decision makers to real-time information has played a key role"... in helping keep the economy in a milder recession, and allowing a quicker comeback after the events of September 11, 2001.
–Testimony of Chairman Alan Greenspan
Federal Reserve Board's semiannual monetary policy report to the Congress Before the Committee on Banking, Housing, and Urban Affairs, U.S. Senate, March 7, 2002.

Commenting on Greenspan's assessment of the real-time enterprise, AMR research concluded, "While the evaluation of needs and technology may seem like a daunting task, moving your enterprise toward a more real-time environment will not only improve the health of your company, but the health of the entire free world as well."

Table of Contents

Preface

In this book, we go under the covers of the buzzwords and hype to examine the many facets that make up the notion of a real-time enterprise. We share insights gained from our experiences on the front lines with pioneering companies that have already recognized what it means to become a process-managed real-time enterprise, and are working intensely to become such. We also assess its implications for business strategy, for our goal is to answer the question of what the real-time enterprise portends for competitive advantage in business.

Along the way we describe some of the enabling technologies that are required to move from concept to reality. But this book is not about those technologies. It's not for programmers or technologists looking for technical guidance or programming recipes. It's about how the Internet is being forged with a new category of software that gives business people control of their business processes to compete for the future—a future that's certainly not business as usual.

When we *do* talk about enabling technology, it's not to distract the business reader, but to show the *substance* beneath the hype of both the real-time enterprise (RTE) and business process management (BPM) buzzwords being bandied about by consultants, IT vendors and the trade press.

This is primarily a book for business people, for at its core it's about how time-based competition can and must be mastered by the company that wants to win in the decade ahead.

Peter Fingar
Joe Bellini
August 2004

Foreword by Dr. Max More

Never mind New Economy vs. Old Economy industries. What matters is if your business enjoys intelligently revised and technologically enhanced business processes. Business process innovation is beginning to move in concert with accelerating technological evolution. Say goodbye to the New Economy; meet the Now Economy. We are witnessing the emergence of *real-time enterprises* (RTEs) that will comprise the bulk of the Now Economy. In the Now Economy, information flows rapidly through supply and demand chains, crossing corporate boundaries, ensuring maximum efficiency and responsiveness.

The ideal vision of the RTE is one of companies where information moves without hindrance, and business processes are continuously monitored and trigger rapid reactions, usually automated according to embedded business rules. RTEs also sense shifts in tastes and practices and respond by offering new products and services. Automated processes easily traverse corporate boundaries, time zones, media and systems. Batch processes and manual input are minimized by ensuring that real-time information among employees, customers, partners and suppliers is current and coherent. The Now Economy is the instantaneous, frictionless economy of economists' legend—the mythical beast that may finally be emerging from the mist. The Now Economy is a web of RTEs that form a virtual supply and demand chain continually seeking information, monitoring, and responding, guided by humans, mostly at the highest strategic level.

An exhilarating, invigorating prospect. But is this vision an accurate, prophetic glimpse of the company of 2010 or merely a flight of fancy? As a strategic business futurist I have seen numerous indications that the vision points in the right direction. But the seeming inevitability and urgency as seen from a technical perspective must be tempered by looking through the lens of the economist and the organizational psychologist. Both strategic business planners and IT executives need to separate hype from happening. The real-time enterprise is already here in embryonic form. Those who ignore the trends will be buried unceremoniously. But so will those who jump too far ahead. Getting the right balance between dogmatic skepticism and reckless optimism will enable executives to form a strategy to ride the leading but not bleeding edge of the Now Economy.

What is it and where is it coming from?

What exactly is the real-time enterprise? A working understanding of the RTE would include these characteristics:

- Process automation bridging distinct enterprise boundaries, media, and information systems;
- Real-time provision and exchange of information with customers, employees, partners, and suppliers;
- Processes that ensure this information is current and consistent throughout the network;
- Event-driven processes forming a sense-and-respond approach that minimizes manual input, batch processing, delays, and inventory; and
- High adaptability.

The real-time enterprise is crystallizing out of a process-rich brew in which swim Web-enabled customer relationship management, supply-chain event management, enterprise relationship management, partner relationship management, content management, customer analytics, business intelligence, optimization, forecasting and simulation. Into the mix we can throw technologies, including application servers, enterprise application integration, Web services, microservers, event routers, enterprise portals, and digital dashboards—and at the heart is a new category of software, the business process management system.

This fertile brew has been struck by the lightening of intense competition, bringing to life the first members of the real-time species. Many of these are existing behemoths with the most adaptive corporate DNA—Dell Computer (supply chain), Wal-Mart, GE (digital dashboards), Cisco (internal monitoring and reporting, one-day closing of finances), FedEx and UPS (tracking and self-service logistics management), Royal Dutch/Shell (using sensors to monitor its oil refineries and properties) and the lesser-known Zara (demand tracking and inventory minimization). The uptake of real-time by these exemplary businesses gives further weight to the view of renowned venture capitalist, Vinod Khosla, who sees real-time as "the business story of the next decade."

What is driving the real-time enterprise?

Five forces are driving us towards the RTE: The first consists of the group of processes already mentioned, from customer and partner relationship management to analytics and content management. The second driver is the renewed emphasis over the last decade on operational excellence through programs such as Six Sigma, re-engineering, value-based management, and the balanced scorecard. The third driver can be seen in the widespread recognition that competition is increasingly not between individual companies but between supply chains. Analysts have referred to aspects of this supply chain competition in discussions of the extraprise, the value chain, the extended real-time enterprise, collaborative production, forecasting, and replenishment (CPFR) and collaborative commerce.

Collaborative commerce creates enormous opportunities for and benefits from real-time information and processes. Corporations within a value chain benefit by:

- Sharing real-time demand- and supply-chain information;

- Manufacturing and distribution planning;
- Joint product development, including synchronized design and skills management;
- Materials sourcing;
- Strategic sourcing of manufacturing, including warehouse and logistics management;
- Customer service, including synchronized customer contact points, analytics, and synchronized and collaborative sales and marketing including channel management;
- Distributed order management, including real-time order status; available-to-deliver information, and automated order handling and routing;
- Logistics management, including available-to-promise information; and
- Warehouse and transportation optimization.

We find the fourth driving force in the rapid development and convergence of emerging technologies from those mentioned above, to those almost-ready for prime time such as ubiquitous computing, and neural network pattern recognition, and some already deployed technologies with a much larger future ahead including RFID (radio-frequency ID) tags, and natural language processing. RFID tags and ubiquitous computing really represent the most visible front of a tsunamic wave of proliferating sensors and actuators tied into real-time applications that experts see leading to smart dust, self-organizing micro-devices, and, ultimately, *smartifacts*—smart materials and intelligent artifacts. The real-time economy will be a world where food squeals if spoiled or tampered with, packages tell what and where they are, warehouses "talk" to each other, trucks converse with logistics and weather systems to optimize routes, important information finds you wherever you are on any device, shelves restock themselves and signal changes in customer tastes, and the integrated customer relationship system of a financial services firm generates a thank-you call to a customer who has just made a big trade.

The fifth driver for real-time comes from the competitive advantages it enables:

- Reduced lead times, improved efficiency and responsiveness;
- Real-time financial reporting (now demanded by Wall Street);
- Lower stock levels;
- Reduced cost per transaction;
- Superior competitive intelligence and demand information;
- Increased responsiveness to customers;
- Reduction in expensive human input;
- Real-time reengineering of processes;
- Better decision-making;
- Improved leveraging of technological improvements;
- Visibility of the extended supply chain;
- Optimization of procurement; and
- Risk management by optimizing purchase decisions under conditions of uncertainty.

Strategizing for the real-time advantage

So real-time is real, it has begun, and its development seems inevitable. But what should you be doing about it and how does it affect your strategy? Some commentators, intoxicated with the real-time idea, have promised sustainable competitive advantages, using disruptive real-time technologies to *cement* market dominance. This is nonsense. Certainly successful early adopters and best practice users will pull ahead. But real time will eventually become just a cost of doing business, a necessary but not sufficient condition for competitive advantage. Just like Six Sigma or re-engineering, real-time enterprises will only sustain a competitive advantage by doing real time really well and, as Fingar and Bellini explain, setting the pace of innovation.

Achieving mastery will be particularly crucial to "value network architects" (Cisco, Dell) who require process excellence even more than customer solutions companies (Amazon, Charles Schwab) or product innovators (3M). One key to real-time mastery lies in clear definition of business processes. Real-timing sloppy or poorly understood processes will work no better than implementing enterprise systems of the past without prior planning. Superbly engineered real-time processes will produce little benefit unless leaders understand cultural dynamics and align incentives to the adoption and use of real time. Frustrating as it may be to the technocrat, the competitive edge will go to those who master organizational psychology and other *soft* skills both within the enterprise and as applied to data flows to and from others in the extended enterprise.

The real-time enterprise promises so much that many businesses will overdo it. Incremental real-timing will almost always trump big-bang implementations. Executives should consider which aspects of their business would benefit most from real time. Smart strategy means understanding what business you are in, exactly how your processes work, where the incentives lie, and which real-timed processes would contribute most to success. It really is time for real time, but start smart, take small steps, and keep your balance.

I invite you to join Peter Fingar and Joseph Bellini on their insightful journey through the world of the real-time enterprise. They will take you under the hype curve to provide the information and insight you need as you prepare your company for competing successfully in the 21st century.

—Dr. Max More
Director of Content Solutions, ManyWorlds
August, 2004

One

The Real-Time Enterprise in Twenty Minutes

KEY POINTS: *During the first fifty years of using computers in business, automation has been focused on record keeping. But, in case you hadn't noticed, that's changing, changing utterly. As we enter the second fifty years of business automation, computers are being deployed in a way that changes how companies do what they do, how they do their work, how they operate and conduct business. Rather than just speed up what companies already do, real-time computer-assisted business processes will bring about deep structural changes and make Operational Transformation the next frontier for gaining and sustaining competitive advantage.*

"Things have changed in a thousand small ways as a result of the Internet—email, online banking, information access, connections among business partners, online procurement... the list goes on. As the cumulative effect of the thousand points of light of today's business Internet reach the stage of total and immediate access, it becomes clear that a new kind of company, the company of the future, will emerge. In fact, it already has. It's the real-time enterprise."

–Peter Fingar, MIT Sloan School Lecture.

There is no doubt something new is going on in business, though it may not be clear exactly what. In the quest for the Next Big Thing in business, you are probably convinced by now that the next big thing isn't about technology. The technology spending craze of the second half of the 1990s is proof enough.

You also know that the search for new productivity and adaptability must center on squeezing out costs while at the same time finding new ways to get closer to your never-satisfied customers whose needs have also greatly changed under the current economic realities. You know you need to look beyond the walls of your company to seek new operational innovations and to sense and respond to new market opportunities. You know you must become more proactive and less reactive to change.

Yet, although many business people have said, "I told you so, the Internet was only a fad whose bubble burst in the dot-com meltdown," you know the Internet has only begun to transform business. You rightly suspect that the anywhere, anytime, anything connectivity of the Internet can enable unprecedented opportunities for innovation and competitive advantage.

But any plans for business reinvigoration will call for information system capabilities that currently do not exist. You may be responsible for creating these capabilities within your organization. The tools at your disposal include current systems, infrastructure, staff and practices. Each of these represents a significant investment and currently provides value. But they are just not up to the task at hand. You know you need more, but more of what? You know all the latest management innovations such as lean manufacturing and Six Sigma. But those methods only help you perfect what you already do in your business, and you know you need to do something new, something you are not already doing, to gain new business advantage.

Again, you reflect on the universal connectivity of the Internet in thinking about the Next Big Thing. There are numerous advanced technologies and techniques that could help you harness the Internet, but which ones? How will they enable you to transform your business? How can they create new sources of competitive advantage? How do you implement them while leveraging your current investments and business practices?

Of course you are still wary of the Internet, for as the millennium clock rolled over to the 21st century, that something new was thought to be the dot-com revolution, where everything business people knew was wrong, for the Internet had supposedly changed the very rules of business. Traditional business fundamentals were thrown out in favor of stratospheric initial public offerings of firms established by twenty-something year old entrepreneurs.

Indeed the Internet had worked magic on public markets and there seemed no end in sight. That is, until the dot-com crash of 2000, where over an 18-month period the sucking sound could be heard when almost three and a half trillion dollars evaporated as financial markets imploded. Many thereafter concluded that the Internet fad was over. Others, like GE's legendary CEO, Jack Welch, concluded that the impact of the Internet on business had just begun, for the Internet wasn't about a Web site or an IPO, it was all about a major business transformation—Operational Transformation. That transformation has just begun and has been heralded by two predominate buzzwords, the *real-time enterprise (RTE)* and *business process management (BPM)*. A businessperson would have to have his or her head in the sand not to have seen these terms in the business press these days. There's lots of hype. But under the hype curves of these new three-letter acronyms a whole new world of gaining and sustaining competitive advantage is unfolding.

The impact of the Internet's universal connectivity doesn't mean a change in *what* goods and services a company provides, nor does it mean the invention of new industries. Those stories belong to the invention of the steam engine, electricity, railroads and other icons that ushered in the Industrial Age. Instead, universal connectivity signals a change in *how* companies deliver their goods and services—that is, how they do what they do, how they and their trading partners accomplish their work; that's what we call *Operational Transformation*. It's about *how work gets done*, and though that may sound a little boring, Operational Transformation is the next frontier of business advantage.

Today, ingrained work patterns linger from traditional business designs that originated with Adam Smith's concepts of specialization and division of labor in the 1776 book, *The Wealth of Nations*. But change companies must, or their competitors who reinvent the way they work will run circles around them. What GE, Wal-Mart, Virgin Group, Toyota, JetBlue, Dell Computer and other often-cited pioneers have done is *change the game in their industries by making deep structural changes, that, in turn, have been made possible by Internet-enabled business process innovation*—they re-invented the very ways they operate their businesses.

Forrester's CEO, George Colony explained the need for Operational Transformation against the backdrop of the universal connectivity of the Internet; "Whether it's the stirrup, the PC, or electricity, technology has always required change in the way humans work. You don't farm the same way with a hoe as you do with a plow. General Motors didn't organize its robotically driven Saturn production line the way Rolls-Royce structured its hand-built assembly process." You don't conduct business the same way with faxes, phone calls, meetings and emails as you do with real-time business processes delivered over the Internet.

Further, Internet-enabled business process innovations are not one-time events. It's the "pace of innovation" that counts in today's global, and often dog-eat-dog, business world. Michael Dell, who has made his fortune by selling commoditized IT products and services, believes a given business process innovation is not the endgame; it's the starting line. As Andrew Park reported in *Business Week*, "Sure, Dell is the master at selling direct, bypassing middlemen to deliver PCs cheaper than any of its rivals. And few would quarrel that it's the model of efficiency, with a far-flung supply chain knitted together so tightly that it's like one electrical wire, humming 24/7. Yet all this has been true for more than a decade. And although the entire computer industry has tried to replicate Dell's tactics, none can hold a candle to the company's results. Today, Dell's stock is valued at a price-earnings multiple of 40, loftier than IBM, Microsoft, Wal-Mart Stores, or General Electric."

"As it turns out, it's how Michael Dell manages the company that has elevated it far above its sell-direct business model. What's Dell's secret? At its heart is his belief that the status quo is never good enough, even if it means painful changes for the man with his name on the door. When success is achieved, it's greeted with five seconds of praise followed by five hours of postmortem on what could have been done better. Says Michael Dell: 'Celebrate for a nanosecond. Then move on.' After the outfit opened its first Asian factory, in Malaysia, the CEO sent the manager heading the job one of his old running shoes to congratulate him. The message: This is only the first step in a marathon."[1]

Welcome to 21st century business, where the winners are agile, mobile and play hardball. They operate their game-changing business processes in real time, following each business innovation with a marathon of process improvement and optimization. They harness the humble, but mighty, *business process* to form global value-delivery systems that provide comprehensive computer-assisted support, from their customers' customers to their suppliers' suppliers, squeezing out both *costs* and *time* throughout a business web of players interconnected by the Internet. They operate 24/7, not only providing customers, employees and suppliers with real time, actionable information; they provide *self-service* operations so that all involved can actually *conduct business*, anywhere, anytime—they can do more than just see actionable information, they can *act* on it. The company, its suppliers and its customers are all employed by the same value-delivery system—they are fused together as one—each playing its part in creating, delivering and consuming economic goods and services. Indeed, Operational Transformation is the next source of competitive advantage, and companies that pursue this new mode of business will become the process-managed, real-time enterprises that prosper in the decade ahead.

Operational Transformation: The Next Source of Competitive Advantage

Years ago, Dr. Michael Porter, Harvard Business School's authority on competition and strategy, concluded that, "Activities, then, are the basics of competitive advantage. Overall advantage or disadvantage results from all a company's activities. The essence of strategy is choosing to perform activities differently than rivals do." But it's not so easy to change the activities a company currently performs, even if these are now dysfunctional work patterns, for ingrained work habits are hard to break. Even with the universal connectivity of the Internet, many companies still operate in the same basic ways they have always operated, coordinating work manually, conducting meetings, shuffling paper and making repeated phone calls to correct even the simplest of errors in day-to-day business transactions.

Meanwhile, others, some of which are highlighted in this book, actually conduct business with real-time business processes that reach across the globe. Using the principles of business process management, they have made deep structural changes in their organizations that make them different. They are *time-based competitors* and are swift to make major course corrections, while delighting their customers day in and day out with *responsiveness*, rolling out innovations with regularity. It's all in how they do what they do, and they clearly have reinvented how they do what they do.

Operational Transformation requires looking outside the walls of a given company and managing the complete value-delivery system, from its customers' customers, to its suppliers' suppliers. While the Internet provides the digital nervous system for the 21st century company, a new category of business process management software provides what's needed to harness that universal connectivity for business advantage. Companies that master real-time business process management can:

- Automate the Primary Activities of the Firm.
- Radically Reduce the Cost of Business Interactions.
- Provide Self-Service That Delights, While Cutting Costs.
- Radically Reduce the Cost of Software While Speeding Up its Development Time.
- Execute on Innovation with Great Speed and Agility.
- Sense and Respond to Demand.
- Make Deep Structural Adjustments.

Automate the Primary Activities of the Firm. Michael Porter's work on competitive advantage separates a firm's primary activities that deliver value to customers, from its support activities that represent the overhead of being in business (paying the rent, paying employees, human resource management and so on). Primary activities are about innovation, sales and marketing, and customer support—all the rest, the support activities, are essentially back-office costs.

During the first fifty years of business automation, rarely were the firm's primary activities the object of automation, for software had not matured to the point where it could address the complex and oft-changing primary activities of the company. The new category of business process management systems changes that. For example, through its Digitization Initiative, GE is intent on reallocating its resources, reducing the back-office to 10% of resource expenditures, with all the rest devoted to its primary activities. In short, for companies that master real-time process management, business automation will, for the first time, bear directly on the *money-making aspects* of the business instead of the *bean counting*. Because it is the uniqueness of a firm's primary activities that distinguish it from competitors, computer-assistance will give companies the tools they need to differentiate by performing their activities in unique ways—the essence of Porter's notion of strategy.

Radically Reduce the Cost of Business Interactions. It's the cumulative costs across the entire value chain that customers see, and those costs are driven as much by information costs as they are in the actual delivery of goods or services. By pushing down information costs of the entire value-delivery system, companies such as Dell have established dominance in their industries. Time is the critical variable in squeezing out costs, for *squeezing out time* can reduce costs such as inventory, overproduction and transaction handling costs. Reducing or eliminating information lag time across the value chain has a positive impact on the bottom lines of all value-chain participants, including customers. Long ago, management luminary, Peter Drucker, observed that it's the new entrant in an industry that reduces overall costs—both direct and indirect—by managing the entire economic chain that comes to dominate. Companies that master Internet-enabled business process management can gain a new capability for managing costs across the entire value-delivery system.

Provide Self-Service That Delights, While Cutting Costs. Advanced techniques of delivering self-service via the Internet can cut costs of customer care significantly because the customer no longer requires a service representative to handle most service-related issues, and a new generation of self-service can increase customer loyalty because response times to problems can be significantly reduced—no more multiple and frustrating visits to touch-tone hell at the call center to solve even the most straightforward request. A new generation of computer-assisted self-service goes well beyond the simple tasks like checking an account balance or transferring funds from one account to another. Today's self-service capabilities provide a collaboration environment so that customers can have a *dialog* with a company to solve issues that were not anticipated and built into so-called Help menus and frequently asked questions and other already-common self-service techniques.

A new generation of self-service software is increasingly capable of becoming a company's Concierge. Smart companies, such as Progressive Insurance, are making their customers as smart as they are by providing quotes from their competitors. Its Concierge knows its customers will check anyway, so it provides a complete service and does the leg work for them, creating trust in the company. Progressive knows that *trust is the foundation for building lasting relationships* with customers and increasing their lifetime value to the company.

The relationship between a company and its customers doesn't end when a good or service is sold; that relationship has just begun, and must continue throughout the consumption of the good or service. Customer care activities are the most significant touch points with customers, for the cost of acquiring new customers is ten times that of selling to an existing, happy, customer. On the other hand, a dissatisfied customer will tell nine others about his or her experience with a company. Indeed, self-service can provide the *double-leverage* of cutting costs while increasing satisfaction. This represents a truly new source of competitive advantage, for it's a sure formula for strengthening customer relationships. As writer Kevin Kelly noted, "The central economic imperative of the Industrial Age was to increase productivity. The central economic imperative of the network economy is to amplify relationships."[2]

Karen Rogers, VP of FedEx.com, gives a sampling of FedEx's ever-growing self-service functionality, "You can locate a FedEx station, get signature proof of delivery, request a courier for pickup, download global trade tools, get forms for shipping international packages, estimate duties and taxes, request invoice adjustments, and connect to the customer service organization."[3]

"Other self-service Web apps include FedExShip Manager, which lets customers centrally manage domestic and international shipping; Global Trade Manager, which helps users estimate duties and taxes on international shipments; and a tool called Alive that lets customers manage and track ground and freight shipments from Asia to the United States. Technology-based innovations—whether new wrist-mounted bar-code scanners for on-the-go workers or the ability to know the contents of incoming packages provided by FedEx's InSight application—are viewed within FedEx as ways to differentiate the company's products and services."

"Only one factor is rated more critical than innovation to the IT team's mission. 'We will differentiate on innovation,' Dottie Berry, a FedEx V.P. says. 'We will dominate on speed.'"[4]

Radically Reduce the Cost of Software While Speeding Up Development Time. The notion of delivering "software as a service" is all the rage in the technology world. Software components are rendered as *services* delivered over the Web. In short, *Web services provide the foundation for a programmable Internet.* Such Web services commoditize common automation tasks, driving down the costs, and making it child's play to combine two or more components for a higher-level purpose (e.g., combining catalog software, with a shopping cart and credit processing to sell goods on the Web).

Just about any form of software can be delivered as a Web service, and, while the software components themselves become commoditized, their combinations become the opposite of a commodity. The situation is like the commodity, the alphabet. Although everyone has access to the alphabet, only those with creativity and skill are able to fashion unique and high-value works of literature. Although everyone has access to Web services, only those with creativity and skill will be able to fashion unique and high-value business processes. That's where business process management software comes in, for it provides the capabilities needed to orchestrate and choreograph Web services into *unique* end-to-end processes that deliver distinctive value to customers.

While Web services commoditize software—and industry *best practices*—business process management software is the secret sauce that can blend software components to let companies perform their activities in infinitely different ways than their rivals—again, the essence of Porter's notion of competitive advantage is to be different. Likewise, industry best practices can be bundled, unbundled and rebundled in unique ways to create innovation practices—*innovation practices* supersede commoditized *best practices* as the way to escape the commoditization trap. That often means harvesting the best practices from different industries for business advantage.

BPMG (bpmg.org) council member, Mark McGregor, describes how best practices can be drawn from several industries to create what he calls *next practices*, "What if you looked to brand-based companies such as Coca Cola for your ideas on marketing, what if you looked at someone like Amazon for your inspiration in building on-line shops for your products and possibly someone like McKinsey as your inspiration for providing service? I am sure you will agree that a company that delivered products to the same quality as a pharmaceutical company and services to the standard of McKinsey, while being as smart at brand awareness as Coca Cola and as easy to buy from as Amazon—would cause more than a few ripples in its marketplace."[5]

Execute on Innovation with Great Speed and Agility. Business innovation is no longer a discrete event; it's now the "pace of innovation" that counts. It's never been easy to transform innovative ideas into action, and ultimately, all innovations can be copied. On the other hand, by the time competitors catch up to the innovators or fast followers, the innovators have pushed the envelope once again, running circles around their competitors. Time and time again, innovations from companies like Toyota, Amazon and Dell are there for all to see, but deep structural changes and other trade-offs make it difficult to imitate or replicate the innovator. Rather than try to catch up with Toyota, in 2004 Ford licensed Toyota's hybrid engine. Rather than try to catch up with Amazon, Borders Books outsourced its entire online operation to Amazon.

Business innovation is no longer an episodic, one-time event; it's the launching pad for a stream of follow-on innovations, and savvy innovators use real-time business process management to *execute on innovation* and to gain the *agility* they need to increase the *velocity of innovation*. They set the pace of innovation to stay ahead of the competition. *The ability to execute on innovation is at least as important as the innovation itself,* and in today's technology-dependent business environment the bond between innovation and execution can only be sealed with real-time business process management.

Sense and Respond to Demand. Wal-Mart is notorious for many of its hardball business tactics, but one of the more surprising aspects of this 800-pound industry gorilla is its willingness to share demand information in real time with its suppliers and their suppliers. This willingness isn't to be mistaken for an act of altruism; it's an act of business acumen.

By beaming demand signals in real time to all its suppliers, Wal-Mart enables the entire value chain to respond to actual demand, rather than to forecast. Forecasts, by definition, are wrong. It's this information chain on steroids that allows products to flow from manufacturer to consumer without being unduly imprisoned in Wal-Mart warehouses. The *make-to-demand* business model of the real-time enterprise is a source of competitive advantage that supersedes the forecast-buy-sell model, the supply-push model of the past, with a radically streamlined demand-pull model of business.

Make Deep Structural Adjustments. The shift from supply-push to demand-pull as a business strategy applies to almost all industries, but *it requires structural changes in organizations and their cultures.* In other words, Operational Transformation is much more than automation or digitizing business processes. Becoming a process-managed real-time enterprise requires that companies adopt new business models which, in turn, require organizational realignment and changes in *mental models* of the people that make up the organization. In the past, people and cultural issues were kept at bay because companies did not have the technological infrastructures for making either rapid or deep structural change. But now, with the advent of the Internet and business process management software, they do. As a result, people and cultural issues have surfaced as *the* critical factors of change.

Business process change and innovation is one side of a two-sided coin. Deep structural adjustments to organizations is the other. Companies that can tightly interlock strategy and organizational alignment to Internet-enabled business process innovation will be able to cross a cultural chasm that others cannot. To address this issue, GE has begun training its senior executives in innovation management, for innovation isn't just some nifty business concept; it demands changes in the very ways of doing business if it's to bring about new sources of competitive advantage. The big challenges are cultural and organizational changes, and these *monumental* challenges must be addressed as such.

Offer Product Services. Because consumers want solutions, not products (they really want a hole, not a drill), smart companies have transformed from just selling products to selling product services. General Motors no longer just sells cars; it sells *a safer, easier and more productive ride* with its OnStar technology and services. GE has grown from a product-based company into a services company that also makes great products. Seventy percent of GE's revenue comes from services and, increasingly, from product services. Two decades ago, when Jack Welch took the helm, only 15 percent of GE's revenues came from services. Welch noted in a 2001 shareholder's meeting that product service at GE today is as high-technology as anything the firm does.[6] Smart companies are embedding information and information services into their products, e.g., telephones are becoming Web browsers. But, as Dr. More noted in the Foreword, that's just the beginning of some already deployed technologies with a much larger future ahead; a future where companies will sell product services and smart products.

Note: You may want to read Appendix A: "The Myths and Realities of the Real-Time Enterprise" next to compare and contrast what you may have read in the business press or heard from various media; or save that chapter for a recap of the book in contrast to the media stories and accounts.

References.

[1] Park, Andrew, "What You Don't Know About Dell," Business Week, November 23, 2003.

[2] Kelly, Kevin, *New Rules for the New Economy: 10 Radical Strategies for a Connected World*, Penguin Books, 1999.

[3] http://www.line56.com/print/default.asp?ArticleID=4110

[4] http://www.informationweek.com/story/showArticle.jhtml?articleID=17300234

[5] http://www.bpmg.org/articles.php

[6] Chairman Jack Welch's remarks at the firm's annual shareowners meeting in Atlanta, GA, April 25, 2001.

Two

Competing On Time

KEY POINTS: *In 1988, Boston Consulting Group's George Stalk clearly articulated how Japanese manufacturers used the secret sauce of 'time' as a source of competitive advantage. Fifteen years later a new technology, called Business Process Management Systems, emerged that, for the first time ever, made it possible to harness the universal connectivity of the Internet to engage in time-based competition with great agility, unencumbered by rigid IT systems. Companies that master this new competitive weapon will prosper in the decade ahead.*

Time is the scarcest resource and unless it is managed nothing else can be managed.—Peter F. Drucker, *The Effective Executive*, 1993.

In his 1988 *Harvard Business Review* article, "Time—The Next Source of Competitive Advantage," George Stalk made an interesting observation about the very nature of competitive advantage: *"Like competition itself, competitive advantage is a constantly moving target.* For any company in any industry, the key is not to get stuck with a single simple notion of its source of advantage. The best competitors, the most successful ones, know how to keep moving and always stay on the cutting edge. Today, time is on the cutting edge. The ways leading companies manage time—in production, in new product development and introduction, in sales and distribution—represent the most powerful new sources of competitive advantage. Cutting-edge companies today are capitalizing on time as a critical source of competitive advantage: shortening the planning loop in the product devel-

opment cycle and trimming process time in the factory—
managing time the way most companies manage costs, quality
or inventory. In fact, as a strategic weapon, time is the equivalent of money, productivity, quality, even innovation. While
time is a basic performance variable, management seldom monitors its consumption explicitly—almost never with the same
precision accorded to sales and costs. Yet time is a more critical
competitive yardstick than traditional financial measures. Time
is a fundamental business performance variable."[1] Of course,
Stalk wasn't the first to recognize the value of time in business:

- Benjamin Franklin: "Time is money."
- Henry Ford: "Time waste differs from material waste in that
  there can be no salvage."

Stalk did, however, articulate time as a competitive variable
at a time when Japanese firms were beating the pants off their
competitors around the globe. His follow-on book with Thomas Hout, *Competing Against Time,*[2] documented the magic Japan
had used to wrest competitive advantage—out of thin air. After
World War II, Japan's advantage was low wages, but when
wages rose, the Japanese transformed to compete on scale with
the management notion of the *focused factory.* But competing on
scale led to ruthless price competition, falling margins and the
need to narrow product lines to maintain economies of scale.
Henry Ford once said, "An American can have a Ford in any
color, so long as its black." But just as General Motors taught
the Ford Motor company that *variety* is a key to advantage and
healthy margins, the Japanese manufacturers began to move to
the notion of the *flexible factory* to compete on variety.

The problems associated with producing a wide variety of
products are associated with setup, materials handling, inventory
and many of the overhead costs of a factory. Stalk and Hout

pointed out that as variety increases, costs increase usually at a rate of 20% to 30% per unit each time variety doubles.

So, what creative companies like Toyota did was to figure out, with great effort, how to blend scale and variety costs where the two yielded the least total cost of manufacturing. In tough economic times, they could pare down their product lines to reduce variety costs, and in good times they could ramp up high-margin product varieties. Toyota's production system became the reference model. Stalk explained, "With its emphasis on just-in-time production, total quality control, employee decision making on the factory floor, and close supplier relations, the Toyota system gave the many Japanese manufacturers who adopted it in the mid-1970s a distinct competitive advantage. In fact, what Toyota, Honda and other variety-driven companies pioneered was time-based competitiveness. They made *structural changes* that enabled their operations to execute their processes much faster. As a consequence, time became their new source of competitive advantage."

Although Toyota introduced the time-based factory, it had other lessons to learn, for there is more to business success than just manufacturing response times. Other parts of the overall value-delivery system are just as important. Stalk returned to the story of Toyota to elaborate this point, "By the late 1970s, leading Japanese companies were finding that inefficient sales and distribution operations undercut the benefits of their flexible manufacturing. Toyota, which at that time was divided into two separate companies, Toyota Motor Manufacturing and Toyota Motor Sales, again makes this point. Toyota Motor Manufacturing could manufacture a car in less than 2 days. But Toyota Motor Sales needed from 15 to 26 days to close the sale, transmit the order to the factory, get the order scheduled, and deliver the car to the customer. By the late 1970s, the cost-conscious, com-

petition-minded engineers at Toyota Manufacturing were angry
at their counterparts at Toyota Motor Sales, who were frittering
away the advantage gained in the production process. The sales
and distribution function was generating 20% to 30% of a car's
cost to the customer—more than it cost to make the car!"

"Finally, in 1982, Toyota moved decisively to remedy the
problem. The company *merged* Toyota Motor Manufacturing and
Toyota Motor Sales. Within 18 months all the Toyota Motor
Sales directors retired. Their jobs were left vacant or filled by
executives from Toyota Motor Manufacturing. The company
wasted no time in implementing a plan to cut delays in sales and
distribution, reduce costs, and improve customer services. The
old system, Toyota found, had handled customer orders in
batches. Orders and other crucial information would accumu-
late at one step of the sales and distribution process before dis-
patch to the next level, which wasted time and generated extra
costs. To speed the flow of information, Toyota had to reduce
the size of the information batches. The solution came from
company-developed computer systems that tied its sales people
directly to the factory scheduling operation. By 1987, Toyota
had reduced system responsiveness to eight days, including the
time required to make the car. The results were predictable:
shorter sales forecasts, lower costs and happier customers."

The competitive value of variety and the variety wars continue to this day. As this book was being written in 2004, Chevrolet was advertising on television that it is turning out ten new
models every 20 months; "The new Chevrolets keep coming."
Chevrolet understands its customers' demands for variety, and
intends to meet those demands. Clearly, Chevrolet has become
a time-based competitor, and refreshed its core business processes to meet this strategic goal.

A review of the many transformation stories in Stalk and

Hout's must-read book reveals the tremendous effort and resources that have been needed to adopt a time-based approach
for managing the work of companies. In the Toyota story, for
example, a radical transformation was made by *restructuring* the
organization. Restructuring organizations, co-locating research
and production facilities, and other forms of radical change,
have always consumed tremendous amounts of resources, energy and effort—that is, until now. With the advent of the
Internet and a new breed of software, business process management systems, both *strategic restructuring* and *tactical operational
response time* can be achieved, in large part, *virtually!*

- *GE's Jeff Immelt on Strategic Restructuring:* When describing his
  company's Digitization Initiative at MIT's 2003 Emerging
  Technologies Symposium, GE's Jeff Immelt, emphasized the
  strategic restructuring issue, "Information technology allows
  us to run the company differently. It allows us to make massive resource allocation decisions so that we can now apply
  more resources to things that we think are going to grow the
  company for the long term." In fact, some observers describe BPM as a new form of Mergers & Acquisitions, for it
  allows companies to restructure inter-company operations
  without all the legal, financial and hassle factors, while sharing risks and rewards. In a minute, we'll expand on the notion of a virtual merger with the story of the Virgin Group.

- *Alan Greenspan on Operational Response Time:* "The same forces
  that have been boosting growth in structural productivity
  seem also to have accelerated the process of cyclical adjustment. Extraordinary improvements in business-to-business
  communication have held unit costs in check, in part by
  greatly speeding up the flow of information. New technologies for supply-chain management and flexible manufacturing imply that businesses can perceive imbalances in inventories at a very early stage—virtually in real time—and can cut

production promptly in response to the developing signs of unintended inventory building." In a moment, we'll expand on response time with the story of the Progressive.

How these Immelt and Greenspan outcomes are accomplished is all about business process change and Operational Transformation.

The dot-com crash wasn't all bad, for what it signaled was that the *tinkering phase* of the business Internet had come to an end, and that pioneering businesses could apply the expensive lessons learned to seek new ways of harnessing the Net for competitive advantage. *Indeed, we are not at the beginning of the end, we are at the end of the beginning of global e-business, a brave new world of time-based competition powered by business process innovation and Operational Transformation.*

Cutting to the chase, what smart companies have learned is that the universal connectivity of the Internet can be applied to *how* a company accomplishes its *work processing* and *strategy execution* to achieve operational innovation by squeezing out time. But that outcome won't just magically happen; it requires a new kind of business automation that later we lightheartedly call the *Work Processor*, the Strategy-Execution machine. In IT industry terms, the Work Processor is a new category of software called *business process management* systems. This category is so important, for the time-based reasons we have just described, that every major IT provider, from Microsoft, to IBM to SAP to Oracle to the independent software vendor, is developing or already offering these new BPM systems.

This shift to business process management is the biggest change in the use of business automation since the first commercial computer was delivered on June 14, 1951, for it shifts the use of computers from record-keeping machines to machines that directly support the actual conduct of outward-facing business activities—machines that power time-based competition. *So, while the notion of time-based competition isn't new, the capability to execute on this management innovation with computer-assisted support is.* Two landmark books capture the *what* and the *how* of time-based competition:

- 1990, the What: *Competing Against Time: How Time-Based Competition is Reshaping Global Markets*, by George Stalk and Thomas M. Hout, Free Press.

- 2003, the How: *Business Process Management: The Third Wave*, The Breakthrough That Redefines Competitive Advantage for the Next Fifty Years, by Howard Smith and Peter Fingar, Meghan-Kiffer Press.

The Stalk and Hout book describes the business case, and the Smith and Fingar book describes the BPM breakthrough for actually doing time-based competition in the 21st century. Fusing the two concepts of time-based competition and business process management together is encapsulated in the notion of the real-time enterprise. We connect the dots in this book, demonstrating that the real-time enterprise isn't the invention of time-based competition; it is its unleashing.

Consider a very mundane business term, *inventory*. According to engineering consultants, Strategos, "The best way to reduce inventory is to improve processes, facilities, quality, scheduling and setups. Firms with outstanding inventory performance excel on other dimensions, such as customer service, delivery and productivity. Excessive inventory is not a problem nor is it evil; it is only an effect. Just as obesity and fat are not problems; only symptoms of poor diet and insufficient exercise. The fundamental causes of high inventory, like the fundamental causes of obesity lie deeper. Since inventory is a result rather than a root cause, attempts to attack it directly will fail. Such attempts may bring temporary reductions. Or they may produce unintended results such as increased defects or increased delivery *time*. High turnover is thus important for at least three reasons: 1) Releases Cash, 2) Encourages Superior Performance, and 3) It's Expensive To Carry Excessive Inventory. Again, the best way to reduce inventory is to improve processes, facilities, quality, scheduling and setups"[3]—all these variables are about *time*.

Inventory turnover isn't king just in manufacturing; it's obviously the key to the distribution trades as well. Sears was once the retailing king with scale, money and real estate, but it didn't compete on time—Wal-Mart did. Sears replenished its stock once every two weeks. Wal-Mart installed a private satellite network to transmit the demand signal from its stores to its suppliers and distribution centers in real time. Furthermore, it designed its distribution centers so that its trucks would have to travel no more than one day to reach any given store. It's key to note that Wal-Mart uses the term distribution center, not warehouse. Goods sitting in warehouses aren't earning money; they are sitting still, costing money. Wal-Mart's distribution centers use a technique of cross docking where supplier trucks arrive at one side of the center and goods are offloaded and reloaded directly into outbound Wal-Mart trucks, speeding their valuable cargo to the retail stores. As a result, Wal-Mart has been able to replenish its stores twice a week.

Today, Wal-Mart is earth's largest retailer. It's also the world's largest employer. In 2003, 7.5 cents of every dollar spent in any store in the United States went to Wal-Mart. According to *Fast Company*, Wal-Mart is bigger than ExxonMobil, General Motors and General Electric. It does more business than Target, Sears, Kmart, J.C. Penney, Safeway and Kroger combined. And the company is still growing—rapidly. In fact, executives boast it has just scratched the surface. Wal-Mart plans to open about 50 to 55 new discount stores and 220 to 230 new Supercenters for fiscal year 2004.

Business editor, Bob Mook, has speculated on what this ferocious time-based competitor might become: "I have a premise for a science-fiction novel. Set in the not too distant future, it involves a small band of maverick businesspeople who battle the world's dominant employer. The company—let's call it Mal-Wart—enslaves about 99 percent of the global population through its manufacturing, distribution and retail operations. But that's not all. Mal-Wart controls all major industries: building and construction, banking and finance, energy, transportation, technology, health care and media. The company rules these sectors with a brutal efficiency that obliterates the competition and leaves oppressed workers across the globe overworked and underpaid as prices for goods and services plunge lower and lower. Anyway, to make a long story short, the scrappy businesspeople lose. You expected a happy ending?"

"Manufacturers of everything from bras to bicycles have had to lay off employees and shut down U.S. plants to meet the retailer's growing price demands. Given Wal-Mart's aggressive growth strategy, expect to find Wal-Marts inside of Wal-Marts someday. All will become Wal-Mart. It is the corporate equivalent of 'Star Trek's' Borg: 'You must assimilate ... resistance is futile.'"[4] Time-based competition is indeed powerful, even scary, stuff, for as Wal-Mart demonstrates, *time is a competitive variable that amplifies all other competitive variables.*

Time-based competition doesn't apply only to manufacturing and distribution of physical goods; it also applies to intangibles. In 1994, the insurance company, Progressive, introduced a fleet of 2,600 Immediate Response® vehicles fitted with laptop computers, intelligent software, and wireless access to the Internet and the company's claims department. In its own words, "Progressive's vision is to reduce the human trauma and economic costs associated with automobile accidents. We do this by providing our customers with services designed to help them get their lives back in order again *as quickly as possible.* Our unique combination of 24-hour policy service and Immediate Response claims service offers customers a refreshing alternative to traditional nine-to-five insurance companies."[5] As quickly as possible? Instead of the 7-10 day adjuster response time of the traditional nine-to-five insurance companies, Progressive's goal is now nine hours!

What did customers of other insurance companies think of Progressive's response times? The company grew from being a $1.3 billion company in 1991 to $11.9 billion in 2003 by competing on time. Just as *price elasticity* used to be the measure of customer demand, Progressive learned that *time elasticity of price* provides a means to simply steal customers away in what is otherwise a matured, domestic commodity market.

Progressive didn't rest on its time-based laurels. It continued to innovate with time as a means to get closer to its *future* customers by considering the needs of time-strapped consumers in today's hectic world. As we briefly mentioned earlier, in 1994, Progressive began offering free rate comparison services, tapping publicly available information, making it the only company to offer apples-to-apples comparison rates from Progressive and up to three other companies. This of course saves the consumer tremendous amounts of time in shopping for the best rates. Many times Progressive does not have the lowest rate and turns business to a competitor. In such cases, however, Progressive builds the reputation of its brand. In addition, it adds considerable information on the insured to its database, including demographic information, which company had the lowest rate, what the lowest rate was, and contact information for the customer who chooses to purchase insurance elsewhere. With time on its side, Progressive constantly monitors the rates of its competitors in order to provide this service, and it is able to re-establish contact with the insured when its rate becomes more favorable. Progressive's strategy illustrates the point that by saving their prospective customers time, the company also builds on and reinforces another key competitive variable—trust, the true foundation for building valuable relationships.

In addition to the insurance industry, we have witnessed the opening volleys in a war for owning the total customer relationship through excellence in logistics. The war is all about time, so much so, that time itself is sold as "the product." FedEx invented express distribution three decades ago based on the value proposition that presents itself when the time-value of an item is significant in proportion to the overall value of the item.

Although we have argued that *time value* is an essential variable in modern economics and is a critical component of customer service, thirty years ago, the idea seemed far fetched. When a former crop-duster pilot, Fred Smith, wrote his 1965 college term paper proposing reliable overnight delivery service, Yale University professor, Challis Hall, read the 12-page paper, thought about the hub-and-spoke idea it contained and promptly gave it a less than favorable grade: "The concept is interesting and well-formed, but in order to earn better than a 'C,' the idea must be feasible." Undaunted, Smith went on to start a company based on the idea of selling *time* and founded the Federal Express Corporation in 1971.[6] In 2003, FedEx had revenues of $22.5 billion, and had already positioned itself to lead the way in the burgeoning China market. FedEx now serves 190 cities in China, and plans to expand service to 100 additional cities within the next five years. It seems that globalization, advanced Internet technologies and time-based competition are indeed well-formed business ideas, Professor Hall.

But there's more to this story, for the role of the warehouse has changed from being a holding bin to an assembly plant. Warehouses have become what the *New York Times* calls the "factory of the future."[7] Will FedEx's "flying warehouses" become flying assembly plants as time continues to be squeezed out of customer-driven supply chain?

Logistics companies that sell "time," like all companies, are always looking for new sources of business that they can leverage with their core competency of squeezing out time. Geoffrey James reported in the July 2004 issue of *Business 2.0* magazine: "When people think of UPS (UPS), they usually think of brown delivery trucks and guys in shorts dropping off packages. They do not think of laptop repairs. But that's exactly the business UPS has decided to enter. Toshiba is handing over its entire laptop repair operation to UPS Supply Chain Solutions, the shipper's $2.4 billion logistics outsourcing division. UPS will send broken Toshiba laptops to its facility in Louisville, Ky., where UPS engineers will diagnose and repair defects. Consumers will notice an immediate change: In the past, repairs could take weeks, depending on whether Toshiba needed components from Japan. But because the UPS repair site is adjacent to its air hub, customers should get their machines back, as good as new, in just a matter of days."[8]

Another well understood and established industry is telecommunications. Let's return to the notion of using business process management to accomplish a "virtual merger" and time-based competition. In his April 2004 article, "Look, Ma— No Towers," David Ewalt reported how Virgin has built a small but growing mobile-phone business without deploying cellular infrastructure: "Just over a year and a half ago, in New York's Times Square, an explosion of confetti, a bevy of nearly naked dancers, and pounding music heralded the birth of Virgin Mobile USA. The scene—a stunt characteristic of Virgin Group founder Richard Branson—culminated with the charismatic Brit descending from the heavens on a crane, clad in a faux-nude bodysuit. Virgin Mobile in the last 18 months has surged from nothing to become a viable choice for mobile-phone service. And it has never installed a single cell tower. Virgin Mobile last month released numbers that showed it now has about 1.8 million subscribers, which puts it among the top 10 U.S. mobile providers. Between the third quarter of last year and the recently completed fourth quarter, Virgin's customer base grew more than 50%. 'We're very pleased,' Virgin's CIO, Mike Parks says. 'We're exceeding our own expectations.'"

"Those [expectations] were pretty high to start with, given the company's historical pattern of success as it evolved from a music retailing outfit to a global airline to a thriving chain of retail stores selling Virgin-branded cola, cosmetics, credit cards, and condoms. Its British mobile-telecom operation, Virgin Mobile Telecoms Ltd., is that country's fifth-largest provider, with 3.7 million subscribers, and is valued at more than $2 billion—a good result for a $75 million investment."

"It took leading mobile providers such as AT&T, Cingular, and Verizon many hundreds of millions of dollars to get where they are today, as well as years of infrastructure development and deployment. It took Virgin Mobile four months to go from 'nothing to making prepaid phone calls on a nationwide network,' says Parks, who has been with the company since the start. 'That's an incredibly short period of time.'"

Virgin forged relationships with Sprint PCS to host their cellular connections and deployed smart integration software to connect their *business processes* to network operators. "The biggest challenge for virtual cellular operators selling prepaid plans is working in a real-time world, all the time. 'You need to take the customer's money, post it to their account, prompt for more money ... everything's happening *now*,' Parks says. 'Most people who are involved in cellular don't live in the now. Usually, you complete a phone call, and I send you a bill in 30 days.' Virgin Mobile's arrangement with Sprint calls for it to pay the network provider a monthly sum based on the amount of traffic it sends to the network, but it also has to communicate with Sprint on a real-time basis when it comes to passing data relating to call authorizations and time allowances on a caller's plan."

"The first key to making those real-time transactions happen was tying together Virgin Mobile's internal systems, including Siebel Systems customer-relationship-management software, a Screaming Media content-publishing system, and J.D. Edwards accounting applications. When customers dial their phones, the software acts as a transaction broker between the various applications, instantaneously making sure customers have time left in their accounts and authorizing the call."

"Applications from operational support-system vendor Telcordia Technologies Inc. sit atop this environment and are responsible for the real-time transactions between Virgin and Sprint. Telcordia's software—a combination of signaling software and a user database that includes all the customer's account information—sits between Sprint's network and Virgin's financial and other applications. 'It acts as the bank for Virgin,' says Robbie Cohen, senior group VP for wireless, cable, and emerging markets at Telcordia. 'Every customer that Virgin serves is known, the balance they have is known.' The software looks into Virgin Mobile's customer databases to see if a caller has enough money in his account to place a call, debits time from the account as the call proceeds, and alerts Sprint to terminate a call when prepaid minutes run out or the caller hangs up. By breaking into the top 10 in 18 months, Virgin Mobile has shown that it's an effective way to compete against rivals that spent billions of dollars to build cellular networks."[9]

In the same industry, telecommunications, at least one incumbent demonstrates what happens if a company doesn't compete on time. An April 17, 2004, headline in the *New York Times* tells the story, "Slow to Adapt, Nokia Loses Market Share in Latest Cellphones.[10] Nokia, the world's largest mobile phone maker, paid a heavy price on Friday for missing the trend toward stylish clamshell phone handsets, denting its vaunted reputation as the arbiter of cellphone chic. Biting into Nokia's market share, the company's hottest rival, Samsung Electronics, reported soaring profits, while Nokia forecast a further slump. Nokia shares touched a 13-month low as investors began looking toward other cellphone makers regarded as likely to tap into a market of fleeting fashions and fickle loyalties. 'No brand can stay cool forever,' said Peter Firstbrook, an analyst with the META Group, a technology research consultant firm in Stamford, Conn. 'Nokia has been slow to adapt.'"

"Most striking, however, is that recent declines in Nokia's share price mean that Samsung's market capitalization has now overtaken Nokia's as the largest for any technology company outside the United States. The shift in part reflects Samsung's broader product line, which includes memory chips and flatscreen displays as well as high-end mobile phones, at a time when all those products are fetching high prices." In traditional economics, *price elasticity* measures show just how much consumers are willing to pay before demand drops off. In time-based competition, the *time elasticity of price* shows that consumers are willing to pay a price premium to buy an innovation in the *now*. Time-based competitors reap rewards commensurate with their speed.

"Nokia has obviously made some major mistakes," said Urban Ekelund, an analyst with Redeye, a private research company in Stockholm. "Firstly, they haven't launched clamshell products, which came to Asia one and a half years ago. And second, they haven't launched products with good color screens and cameras. By contrast, Samsung has been 'focusing on high-end products," Mr. Ekelund said in a telephone interview, while "Nokia has been focusing too much on the low end," and on emerging economies rather than richer markets like the United States. This validates the point that the followers are left to battle it out as low-margin commodity players while the innovators move on to new hunting grounds.

"In a television interview, Jorma Ollila, Nokia's chief executive, said, 'There were some changes in the products of our competitors, and we were not as swift in moving.' 'As you get bigger, you become the target, and it becomes harder to move quickly,' said Mr. Firstbrook of the META Group. "Nokia became bigger not necessarily because they were best, but because everyone else was stumbling. Now there is more competition, and the competition is getting better. Nokia is a bit of a dinosaur in terms of changing direction."

These telecommunication industry stories highlight the two major aspects of time-based competition, *Response Time* (where Lag Time, Lead Time, Inventory Turnover and Cycle Time must be squeezed out in order to meet never-satisfied consumer demands) and *Restructuring Time* (where Reorganization, Asset Reallocation, Business Process Change and Strategy-to-Execution Time are paramount management challenges).

Before turning our attention to the many dimensions of the real-time enterprise, let's turn to Stalk and Hout to summarize the fundamentals of time-based competition. "Companies that operate more efficiently and responsively than their competitors have better-designed and better-managed systems. Thus the quality of their systems is often a much or more important for

their sustainable advantage as are their products and services."
In BPM terms, *the product is the process.*

"Until recently, innovations in business strategy were episodic. A major discovery, usually technology based, would upset
the balance of an industry, and corporate fortunes would shift.
For example, in transportation the railroads drew hoards of
crowds from river boats and horse drawn overland transportation companies in the 1880s only to lose customers in the mid-
twentieth century to trucking firms. Similarly, coal companies
replaced wood companies in the market and were themselves
upstaged by oil companies. Today, however, episodic changes in
business strategy are fewer and they are being supplanted by
evolutionary change—a continuum of change, not only in
physical technologies but in managerial technologies as well."

"Time-based competitors: Compress time to manufacture
and distribute their products; Significantly cut time to develop
and introduce new products; Significantly cut inventory
throughout the value-delivery system; Lever all other competitive differences with the advantages in *response* time. Yielding:
Productivity increases; Premium prices; Risks are reduced; and
Share is increased. Using the following methods: Choosing time
consumption as a critical management and strategic parameter;
Using responsiveness to stay close to their customers, in creas-
ing customers' dependencies on them; Directing their value-
delivery systems to their most valuable customers; Setting the
pace of innovation in their industries; Growing faster with
higher profits than competitors; and Baffling their competitors
(market disruptions). To do this, time-based competitors: Make
their value-delivery systems 2-3 times more flexible and faster
than their competitors; Determine how customers value variety
and responsiveness, focus on those with the greatest sensitivity
and price; and Have a strategy for surprising competitors with

the company's time-based advantage. Senior management must shift its focus from cost to time, and its objectives from control and functional optimization to providing resources to compress time throughout the organization [and entire value-delivery chain]. Time is the number one [competitive factor]!"

"Forecasting is always, by its very nature, wrong. Better forecasts and longer lead times aren't the answer. Only way to break this cycle is to reduce the consumption of time throughout the value-delivery system. The challenge of becoming a time-based competitor is as much a white-collar task as it is a factory task, because time delays appear anywhere in the value-delivery system. Companies must measure time consumption the way companies now measure cost consumption. Innovation means more than just new products; it means new services and ways of doing business as well—FedEx-overnight delivery; Delta-hub and spoke. Innovations along any dimension can upset competitive balances by enticing customers to switch and by putting competitors on the defensive."[11]

A Final Lesson from Nature

Polar bears have a unique ability to smell (sense) through thin ice to locate their favorite prey, the seal. But they also know that their prey is an elusive target, and that it's knowing exactly when to pounce (respond) through the ice that counts. Pouncing too soon, before maneuvering to the right spot where the ice will break cleanly, or pouncing too late after competitive bears have spotted the prize, will surely mean lost opportunity and continued hunger. It's all in the timing—it's time-based competition for survival in a harsh world.

McKinsey & Company maintains that competitive advantage consists of the progress a company makes as its competitors, paralyzed by confusion, complexity and uncertainty, sit on the sidelines.[12] The key is to be ready to pounce on an opportunity as soon as the company can realign the business processes of its value-delivery system, not just to be the first mover, but also to be able to swim hard once it has broken the ice with innovation. Having caught up with the bear and joined in the melee, competitors will only have remnants of the prize to fight over while the innovator moves on, scouting for new opportunities to surprise both its prey and its competitors.

In the world of business, a company cannot hope to compete in the arena of time-based competition if it continues to have non-value-added processes, disconnected departmental hand-offs, or broken or anemic business processes. An anemic bear simply cannot compete in the harsh real world—time-based competition demands Operational Transformation through business process innovation.

References.

[1] Stalk, George, "Time—The Next Source of Competitive Advantage," *Harvard Business Review,* July-August, 1988.

[2] Stalk, Jr. and Thomas Hout, *Competing Against Time, Free Press, 1990.*

[3] http://www.strategosinc.com/inventory.htm

[4] http://www.coloradoan.com/news/stories/20040215/business/419798.html

[5] http://www.progressive.com/newsroom

[6] Science and Technology Quotes located at
http://busboy.sped.ukans.edu/~adams/sciquot.htm

[7] Saul Hansell, "Is This the Factory of the Future?" *New York Times,* July 26, 1998.
http://www.muhlenberg.edu/depts/abe/business/miller/proddat/tjy25ops.htm

[8] http://www.business2.com/b2/web/articles/1,17863,655497,00.html

[9] http://informationweek.com/story/showArticle.jhtml?articleID=18900823

[10] http://www.nytimes.com/2004/04/17/business/17phone.html

[11] Stalk, Jr. and Thomas Hout, *Competing Against Time, Free Press, 1990.*

[12] McKinsey Quarterly, 2002 Number 2, *Just-in-Time Strategy for a Turbulent World*

Three

How Work *Works* in Business

KEY POINTS: *Unfortunately, most of the information about the real-time enterprise and business process management is shrouded in technical jargon and Harvard-speak. To crack that shell, and in the spirit of PBS television shows on "how things work," let's start our discussion with some simple, even pedestrian language, and have some lighthearted fun as we explore how work works in business. This discussion lays the foundation for how Operational Transformation is made possible by the universal connectivity of the Internet and business process management systems that exploit that connectivity—that's the gist of the revolutionary business SEx machine.*

Architecture. An architecture is the arrangement and connection of components to bring about an overarching, identifying structure that is rationalized to provide best fit for its purpose. All structures have an architecture whether or not that architecture is explicitly or implicitly defined. Considering classical building architecture, *good* architecture is difficult to define, but you'll know it when you see it.

Business Architecture. Businesses, too, have a structure, and thus have either an explicit or implicit architecture. Business architectures consist of two major classes of components: tangible capital assets (e.g., land, labor, buildings, cash and equipment) and intangible assets that are structured to carry out the work of the business. What gets interesting is that two companies having identical tangible capital assets produce completely different results. That leaves us with the determining factor, how they structure work by arranging and connecting the work performed by people and automated information systems.

Resulting from the Industrial Age concepts of specialization of labor, the architecture of many businesses is implicit and oriented around "functional specialties" such as engineering, accounting, marketing and so on. This is called functional management. Such business architecture is reflected in the traditional organization chart. The work of an organization, however, spans the white space on the organization chart, and awkward hand-offs and disconnects are typical as work passes from one block on the org chart to another.

In contrast, today's well-oiled companies take a different approach to business architecture. They use *work-oriented architecture*, also known as *process-oriented architecture*, to design their organizations around how work gets done as dynamic, concurrent and often messy work processes that cross the departmental blocks on the org chart—and that cross companies in a value chain. With a work-oriented business architecture, units of work (UOWs) replace the functional department as the basic building blocks for business design (for an in-depth discussion, see Martyn Ould's *Business Process Management: A Rigorous Approach,* The British Computer Society, September 2004). In plain talk, getting work done in a business requires four major architectural entities as shown in Figure 3.1:

1. *Strategy.* This activity is about setting goals, and defining *what* is to be accomplished. Strategy is, of course, all about innovation—innovative new products or services, *or* innovative ways of delivering existing products and services.

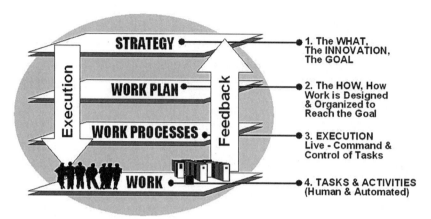

Figure 3.1 How Work *Works* in Business,
a Four-tier Business Architecture

2. *Work Plan.* The work plan is about how work is to be organized for reaching the goal. The work plan includes all the collaborative negotiation and commitment steps, as well as transaction processing steps, that must be carried out to deliver value to customers. Some steps must be designed in sequence, for the input needed for a given step may depend on the output of a previous step. Other steps may be carried out simultaneously, in parallel, if they are not dependent on the completion of prior steps before they can begin. The overall Work Plan must be carefully designed so that it is efficient and can be completed in the minimum amount of time, while independent work carries on within the swim lanes of all participants involved in delivering value to customers. Each contributor works according to its own clock, but those clocks must be carefully synchronized if the overall value-delivery system is to deliver optimal value to customers within the timeframes that customers demand.

3. *Work Processing.* Work Processing is about working the plan. It's the live execution, or live *work processes* of the Work Plan that produces results for customers. As shown, at this level

in the business architecture, work isn't just what any one individual does, for the work that any one individual does depends on others, inside and outside the business. In fact, even the work that a given company does depends on other companies, its suppliers and trading partners. Thus, *work isn't something you do; it's something you process.* Work Processing is the command and control of individual tasks and activities performed by people and computers to produce desired results.

4. *Work.* Work, in this four-tier model of a business, is about the individual, discrete tasks and activities carried out by both people and machines.

Figure 3.2 expands the model and presents a taxonomy of the individual tasks and activities, based on Michael Porter's value-chain analysis. Porter's approach asserts that, by modeling the activities of an organization, it is possible to distinguish *primary* activities, those that contribute to getting the product or service closer to the customer, from activities that *support* primary activities. The result of these overall tasks is value delivered to customers, and the margin or *value* is the difference between what customers are willing to pay and the cost of producing the value. The model provides a framework to analyze the effectiveness of resource use and the competitive capabilities of an organization.

Primary activities are directly involved in the creation of a product or service, its sale and transfer to the customer and after sale support. As shown in Figure 3.2, these include sourcing and material procurement, inbound logistics, operations, outbound logistics, and sales and customer service. Support activities are those that, obviously, support primary activities by providing financial resources, research and development, facilities management, human resources and marketing and advertising.

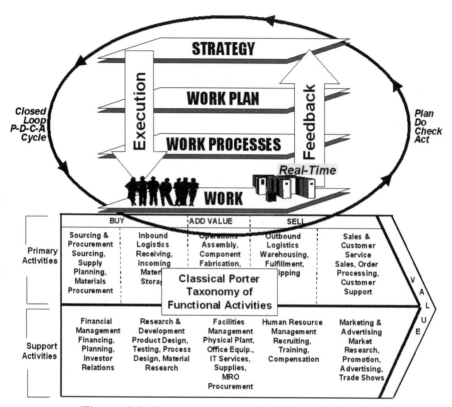

Figure 3.2 How Work *Works* in Business
with Additional Details

Large companies perform thousands of tasks and activities, and chaos would reign if they were not governed in their execution by carefully designed work processes.

A business is a living system, and like all living systems it changes in response to the world around it. At a given point in time, a company creates or revises its business strategy to reflect current market demands. New strategies require new work plans, which, in turn, require restructuring work processes and new work tasks.

The overall flow of change proceeds from *strategy* to *execution*, but doesn't stop there. Strategies and plans are never perfect and economic conditions change, so *feedback of results* is crucial to adjusting strategy and execution. This is the closed-loop of strategy-execution-feedback, and it should flow in real time.

In the 1980s, the total quality management movement was aimed at this never-ending cycle, striving to improve all elements in the process. In simple quality-management terms the strategy-execution-feedback cycle was Plan, Do, Check and Act, or PDCA for short. Today this closed-loop feedback often comes under the label of Six Sigma quality processes. Regardless of the name, companies that want to succeed and *sustain* their competitive advantage must constantly strive to improve their results.

Innovation in strategy and innovation in the execution of innovative strategies are the stuff of market dominance. It's not enough to have innovative ideas; it's the ability to execute on those ideas that counts, making *strategy execution* the critical success factor of any business.

The Internet and Strategy Execution

The capability to add value is the very essence of being a successful business and constitutes an enterprise's core competencies. Adding value does not necessarily mean that the company itself carries out the activities of its core competencies. Dell Computer Corporation, for example, does not *manufacture* computers. Instead, it *assembles* computers. Dell uses the Internet to trigger activities among its suppliers and trading partners that do the actual manufacturing of component parts. Dell's core competency is managing the build-to-order process. Dell goes beyond the internal focus of Porter's analysis and manages the end-to-end, multi-company, value-delivery system.

Figure 3.3 shows a top view of an industry-wide value delivery system. Each participant in the chain, from "my.company" to my.company's suppliers and their suppliers, to my.company's customers and their customers, embody primary and support business processes and resources as previously discussed. Two forces, the demand chain and the supply chain, converge at the point of my.company.

As can be seen in the figure, my.company does not act alone in obtaining materials and services from the supply side of the value chain. Neither does it act alone when facing the demand chain as it may sell direct or through wholesalers or distributors who, in turn, sell to ultimate consumers.

Figure 3.3. Business Process Reengineering (BPR): Reengineering *Inside* the Enterprise

Since the early Nineties, companies have been focused on streamlining the work processes *within* their organizations in response to advances in technology. The introduction of enterprise-wide networks meant that a company could tie together islands of information scattered across business units and individual departments. The enterprise-wide network laid the foundation for deep transformation within companies and the business process reengineering revolution (BPR) ensued. Even if you don't recall the term BPR, far too many people know about its side-effect, *downsizing.*

Companies tore down stovepipes of information contained in individual departments. They connected these islands of information into end-to-end value delivery systems that optimized not individual departments, but overall, end-to-end business processes that deliver value to customers.

The process of tying together islands of information is shown with the connecting lines between individual tasks (the little bars represent Porter's activities). The lines connecting the individual activities of departments represent the enterprise-wide information systems that eliminated many disconnects and redundant activities.

In the early 1990s, business process reengineering provided the management framework, theories and methods for driving change. But, at the time, the digital connections remained inside a single company, and as shown in the figure, each company streamlined its internal work processes, but not necessarily those work processes that crossed company boundaries.

Although the goals were to do things cheaper, better and faster than the competition, the scope of reengineering was inward-focused, paying little attention to the work process interactions beyond the walls of the company. Those were still handled manually with the fax, phone, the field visit, meetings and document passing.

Fast forward from enterprise-wide networks to the anyone-to-anyone, anyone-to-any computer, and any computer-to-any computer connectivity of the Internet. Companies that *get it* and are determined to thrive in the Internet era are redesigning business processes so that they cross enterprise boundaries to eradicate duplicate processes and the ineffective hand-offs between and among enterprises involved in their value-delivery systems.

Virtual corporations and *extended enterprises* are being created that have shared business goals, common planning, and performance management tools. *Industry Process Reengineering (IPR), also known as commerce process reengineering (CPR),* is the new focus for designing and implementing hyper-efficient value-delivery systems that are integrated in real time and jointly owned by suppliers and customers. The competitive notions of "cheaper, better and *faster*" take on a whole new meaning in these 21st century corporations.

Businesses that get it realize that competing for the future is about turning a company, and its entire value-delivery system, over to the command and control of the customer. For example, when a customer goes to Dell for a build-to-order computer, Dell's suppliers and its suppliers' suppliers are linked into the transaction in real time to trigger fulfillment and inventory replenishment. The customer is in the driver's seat initiating activities that ripple throughout the value chain. By implementing a *demand-signal* supply chain, Dell sets records for inventory turns in its industry, and pockets the money squeezed out of traditional inventory carrying costs.

As shown in Figure 3.4, the global connectivity of the Internet extends the four-tier business architecture across the many trading partners that make up a given value delivery systems. My.company's Work Processing now encompasses the shared work activities and tasks of the entire value-delivery system. Real-time links between my.company and its customers and its customers' customers are so tight that they fuse to the point of unity. Ditto, my.company's suppliers. Together with its customers and suppliers, my.company is able to execute on innovation, to the delight of its customers.

The importance of this real-time connectivity was encapsulated by the U.S. Federal Reserve Board's Chairman, Alan Greenspan. "Doubtless, the substantial improvement access of business decision makers to real-time information has played a key role... in helping keep the economy in a milder recession and allowing a quicker comeback."

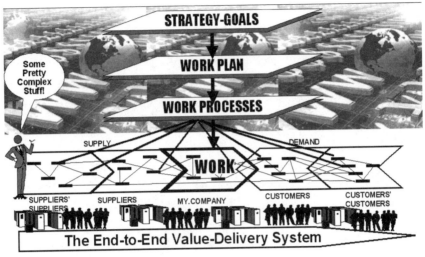

The End-to-End Value-Delivery System

Figure 3.4 How Work Works in the 21st Century

Greenspan recognized the fact that the Internet changes the rules of business from cost-based forms of competition to time-based competition. The speed of the demand signal, and its being heard instantaneously throughout the value-delivery system, becomes as important a competitive variable as classical capital and labor.

But responding to that demand signal is something companies are just now learning to do. It's been tough enough to manage strategy execution within a single company, but now companies must be able to extend their Work Plans and Work Processing across multiple companies and customers. Companies have lots of experience in using business automation for record keeping, but little or no experience applying business automation beyond their four walls, across their entire, end-to-end value-delivery system. Thus, conquering these challenges of time-based competition is the new frontier of business.

The *Work Processor and the* Strategy-Execution Machine

Until now, the work of Strategy, Work Planning, and Work Processing have been largely manual affairs, outside the scope of business automation. But, now the tasks associated with these activities are so complex that new forms of automation must be brought to bear.

An automobile designer faces complex tasks by using a computer-aided design (CAD) system. Disney animators use incredibly advanced animation systems from Pixar to render award winning films. Filmmakers, airplane designers and building engineers have advanced productivity tools to assist in their tasks. But it's not so for the executives, managers and workers who carry out the work of strategy execution in business. To this day, it's still all about manual work processing—faxes, meetings, spreadsheets, phone calls, emails, and the post office.

What's ironic is that companies wouldn't hire a new office worker without providing him or her with a "word processor," but, as shown in Figure 3.5, why don't companies also provide their executives, managers and employees with a "Work Processor?" Later in this book, the term, Work Processor, will be equated with the more sophisticated term, the BPMS or business process management system, and explained in greater detail. But, for now, it can simply be said that to deal with the complexity of cross-company Work Processing, computer-assisted tools are absolutely essential.

The Work Processor is the weapon of choice for engaging in time-based competition. It can be used to squeeze out time from restructuring work processes and delivering value to customers with a sense and respond infrastructure. The Work Processor is the Strategy-Execution (SEx) machine for business.

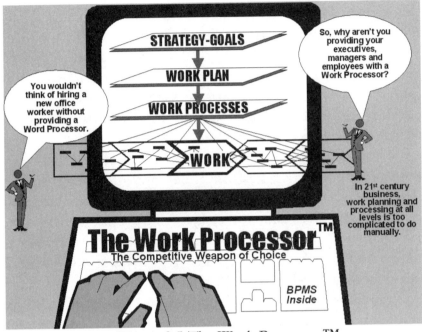

Figure 3.5 The Work Processor™

On the other hand, a Work Processor won't *automagically* make a company a process-managed enterprise. Just as a word processor won't make its user a novelist, the Work Processor is only a tool, albeit a powerful tool. Gaining true benefit depends on mastery of established business disciplines, such as process engineering, voice of the customer, Six Sigma quality and other management innovations. In the past, these disciplines were pretty much manual affairs, and initiatives created to embrace them were piecemeal, scattered throughout pockets of the organization. The Work Processor is the tool that can provide computer assistance for these management disciplines, and it allows a company to take a *holistic approach* to performance improvement and operational innovation.

In addition to mastering the appropriate business disciplines, many companies will have to overcome organizational, cultural and people barriers, for deep structural realignment goes hand-in-hand with Operational Transformation. A tool is just a tool, but without the appropriate tools, companies cannot cope with the end-to-end management of their business processes and reach beyond their walls to improve performance of their overall value-delivery systems.

Because Work Processing must span entire value-delivery systems, Work Processors must be interconnected via the Internet. They must render the appropriate view of work processes for executives and worker bees alike, across multiple organizations. The executive's rendering provides the guidance system, and the other renderings provide the perspective needed for day-to-day decisions and operations.

The Work Processor will become as pervasive as word processors are today, and they will be found on the desks of executives, mid-managers, order-entry clerks and shop-floor journeymen—everyone involved with the work processes of the business, from the boardroom to the traveling salesman. Don't engage in a gunfight with a knife; and don't engage in time-based competition without a Work Processor. Only those that invest rightly in this new form of IT will have the competitive arms they need to set the pace of innovation and win business battles of the future.

Four

What Do "BPM" and "RTE" Actually Mean?

KEY POINTS: *What do BPM and RTE actually mean? It depends on who you ask. Academics, IT vendors, business editors, technicians and management consultants all have their pet definitions. What's important to business decision makers is a working knowledge so that they can make informed decisions without distraction from all the bafflegab.*

The term "BPM" has been adopted in the marketing communications of just about every IT vendor and management consultant, as what comes after the dot-com fiasco. It seems everyone selling IT products or management consulting services has put BPM lipstick on their products and services. Even the IT and financial analysts are having a field day defining BPM to mean whatever they want it to mean.

Although confusion abounds, a handful of useful *working definitions* can bring about some badly needed clarity. Figure 4.1 provides a backdrop for our discussion.

Business Process. The business process (called Work Processing in the last chapter) is the end-to-end *coordinated* set of *collaborative* and *transactional* work activities carried out by both automated systems and people to produce a desired result or achieve a goal. While this definition is simple enough, the coordination of complex sets of activities carried out by independent work participants (humans and machines) is by no means simple.

Business processes are essentially human phenomena, but in today's automated and wired world, automation and technology assistance to amplify human work are indispensable. This technology assistance involves automation of routine transactions and dynamic human collaborations, as suggested in the figure.

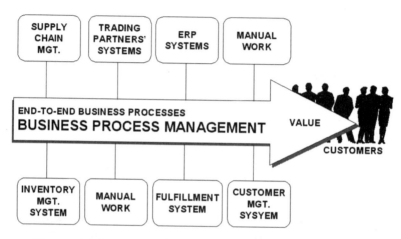

Figure 4.1 Business Processes and Their Management

As we have discussed, in his classic work on value chain analysis, business strategy expert and Harvard professor Michael Porter classified work activities into two types. Primary activities are those that directly touch the customer, while support activities are those that are primarily administrative, keeping the rent paid and the lights turned on. Using Porter's framework, it's the primary, end-to-end customer-touching processes that are paramount to gaining and sustaining competitive advantage. It is these primary business processes that deliver value to customers, and they *are* a company's value-delivery system—all the rest, the support activities, are costs.

While support activities require management attention as means to make a company more *efficient*, primary activities require laser-focus to make a company *effective* in the marketplace.

Business Process Automation (BPA). BPA simply means automating a business process. Since the advent of the first commercial computer in 1951, companies have embraced technology to streamline and speed up their support activities for greater operational efficiency. As far as primary activities, today a number of technology families have emerged for this purpose, including workflow systems and, more recently, Internet technologies such as application servers. While just about any technology can be used to *automate* business processes, the real issue companies face is how to optimize and manage those processes after they have been semi- or fully automated.

To date, business process automation (BPA) *requires delving in technology plumbing and diddling with complex computer programs for each instance of business process change.* That means that technologists, not business people, are required to create or change an automated business process. Companies are so bogged down in expensive and tedious efforts to rewire technology for each process change that, often, needed business change is simply foregone, as it isn't practical or feasible. Thus, business process automation falls short in meeting the needs of time-based competitors and is unable to take companies much beyond where they are today, stuck with rigid business automation systems. Even with a veneer of business process modeling tools made available to business people, technical staff are still required for business process change in most BPA scenarios. But, we'll say it again, the ultimate challenge of business process management is not just the automation of business processes, it's their management thereafter, for change is a certainty. Thus, companies want to go beyond business process automation and on to business process *management* without having to run through the technology gauntlet.

Business Process Management (BPM). BPM is a business discipline or function that uses business practices, techniques and methods to create and improve business processes. From this general definition, just about any process improvement discipline or activity, including reengineering, TQM or Six Sigma quality methods, outsourcing and lean manufacturing, can be considered as BPM. Thus, from an extremely general perspective, BPM has no distinguishing definition at all; it's just about anything that contributes to process improvement—it can mean whatever you want it to mean.

On the other hand, the term BPM has been propelled onto the front pages of the business and technology literature for far more specific reasons. Whether manual or automated, companies have learned that the piecemeal process improvement methods and techniques they have scattered throughout their organizations don't produce breakout results. So, if your manufacturing division uses Six Sigma, and your marketing department uses voice-of-the-customer techniques, without talking to one another, that doesn't mean you have a process-managed enterprise, the kind of enterprise that produces outstanding and sustained business results.

BPM in its contemporary context is a holistic vs. piecemeal approach to the use of appropriate process-related business disciplines that are used to drive business performance improvements, not just across the departments in a single company, but also across multi-company value delivery systems. This approach has only now become practical as a result of the new category of BPM software systems.

BPM Systems. BPM systems are technologies designed for the complete *management*, not just the automation, of business processes, from creating innovative new business processes, to their redesign and improvement over time. BPA, the one-off automation of a business process, is only a part of a complete BPM system. It's the "M" in BPM that really counts, for change is not a one-time affair.

BPM systems (that we lightheartedly called Work Processors) provide computer assistance for supporting all process work such as Six Sigma initiatives; mergers and acquisitions; overriding processes embedded in ERP systems; implementing industry-specific collaboration protocols such as Rosettanet Partner Interface Processes® for the IT industry supply chain; or complying with regulations such as the Sarbanes-Oxley Act.

Automated support systems are absolutely necessary to deal with today's complex business structures and to get beyond the piecemeal approaches to process improvement. Without this automated support, it would take armies of people to take on the real tasks of real-world process work.

BPM Servers. One approach to building BPM systems is to federate preexisting technologies (including workflow, application integration brokers and business rules engines) and add them to an already complex technology stack. Today that technology stack is organized under the banner of *application servers*, software that's part of a three-tier distributed application: the user interface, the business logic, and the back-end databases. Applications servers are often labeled as Internet servers, for their primary use is to connect preexisting systems such as ERP and newer Internet-oriented applications. BPM servers add yet another layer to this already complex technology stack.

The situation is similar to that of the emergence of database systems a couple of decades ago. What are known as hierarchical and networked database systems used pointers and links to keep data elements tied together logically although their physical storage was in quite a different form. They worked, up to a point. When the links were broken, business information systems failed and had to be recovered by reloading the databases. That was certainly no way to run a company's business-critical information systems.

So, along came an innovation. Instead of links and pointers, a researcher at IBM Watson Research Center, Ted Codd, used the mathematics of relational algebra as the foundation for a new kind of database system that obviated the need for complex links and pointers. The relational database management system (DBMS) was so solid and reliable that a whole new breed of applications called enterprise resource planning (ERP) systems emerged that are now the foundation for automation in large and mid-size businesses across the planet. The same level of innovation is needed for business process management if we are to get beyond the already complex technology stack and the additional complexity BPM servers introduce. That innovation is the business process management system (BPMS).

The BPMS Innovation. As before with Ted Codd's innovative approach to data management, Cambridge University's Turing Award winner (the Nobel Prize equivalent for computer science), Robin Milner, took a fresh approach to process management. Like Codd, Milner turned to the mathematics (pi calculus) to find the needed underpinnings for representing and manipulating processes. A DBMS is essentially about storing, processing and managing data. Similarly, a BPMS is fundamentally about storing, processing and managing business processes.

The BPMS is a radical simplification for process work, for it does not add yet another layer to the already complex technology stack—it is simply a *user* of the existing technology stack. Its core capabilities are built from the ground up around business processes, not technology processes. Thus, the tools built atop the BPMS can be designed for business analysts, not just technologists. With BPM servers, the business process is shredded and stored among the various federated technologies. With the BPMS, the business process remains whole, and overcomes the fragility inherent in BPM servers that is similar to the fragility that broke the hierarchical and networked database models. BPMI.org's Howard Smith elaborates, "Business processes are long lived, they exist over time, and thus, have to be persistent. You have to be able to switch off the system and switch it back on again and it's all there. And, processes don't just execute, you need to manage them as they evolve, one way or another, and to differing extents. A BPMS provides a clean model for the stored processes, so that tools can be built above for managing them."

The BPMS is of the process, for the process and by the process; not of, for and by the technology stack. In the early phases of BPM work, companies can get by with BPM servers, and their technical people will be comfortable with the familiarity of that which they already know. Business people will continue to be baffled by the technology stack. But once companies get beyond their initial BPM projects and their process repositories grow exponentially, the complexity of linking preexisting technologies with a BPM server will cause them to hit walls similar to the walls hit by early link-centered database approaches. As companies move beyond the initial tinkering phase of BPM, the need for a *native* business process technology foundation, the BPMS, will become all too clear.

Extending the technology stack with BPM layers is similar to trying to build a skyscraper by stacking a thousand doghouses one atop the other. Skyscrapers need an architecture all their own; business processes need an architecture all their own. The BPMS provides the process-oriented architecture needed to build a process-managed, real-time enterprise.

Process-Managed Enterprise. The leaders of a process-managed enterprise recognize that it's the end-to-end, enterprise-wide business processes that make or break the company. They have a holistic, not piecemeal, definition of enterprise BPM. They also recognize that end-to-end process management is complex and requires not just great management theories, but also requires commensurate support from automation tools.

The process-managed enterprise requires BPM systems to realize the goals they set for holistic process management work. Companies that adopt this perspective often interchange the terms BPM and BPM systems, for the two go hand in glove if management intent is to be translated into execution.

Leaders of a process-managed enterprise understand work-oriented business architecture and design work structures around the end-to-end business processes. They know they need to bring the right tools to the table in order to realize their vision, for business is no longer conducted manually or through time-delayed, batch-oriented information systems. Today's executives want the tools and infrastructure needed to become *time-based competitors*, competing on cycle time, product design time, lead time, time to market, response time, just-in-time inventories and up time. They know that to place time on their side, they need tools that can allow them to create and manage flexible and fine-tuned business processes that can keep up with and even anticipate ever-changing customer demands. Such processes must cross company boundaries and coordinate the multi-company work of the entire value delivery system.

Howard Smith explains the challenge of coordination of work. "In the largely vertically integrated companies of the past, business processes were once thought of as those that could be rigorously scheduled around well-defined roles in carefully designed workflows—routing of work from one role to the next, work that was waiting for a telephone call from a customer, or work that had to be processed at a specific time ("I will expect your call at 10 o'clock"), or work that had to be transferred to a different person because the person who did the first part of the processing got sick or quit before the task was complete. But in today's global, horizontally integrated companies, coordinating business processes is neither as simple nor as linear as portrayed in the tidy world of traditional task management or the overly simplistic process re-design around case workers, typical of the reengineering efforts of the past decade. Today, work management is about coordination, collaboration, negotiation and commitment. Business is constantly changing, messy, unordered and chaotic, and both manual and automated work activities have to progress in parallel. Work is conducted, and coordinated, at all levels, through choreography and orchestration."

Because the multiple companies involved in a single value chain operate on their own clocks, coordination and synchronization can only be accomplished with a robust *information chain* that provides the actionable information each participant needs to optimize the overall flow of work. The ability of systems-of-process to publish or subscribe to real-time transactions, occurring within active business processes, enables organizations to respond to events, such as fraudulent activity in banking or insurance, in real time. This capability also enhances business decision making for time-based activities such as situation-appropriate cross-sell opportunities, based on real-time credit card activity and customer interactions in the contact center.

Automated techniques such as creating a single, complete representation of a customer across all channels and lines-of-business, complex account opening, change of address across multiple lines-of-business, or managing lost or stolen credit cards, are example capabilities of real-time systems-of-process.

According to consumer relationship management expert and CEO of Chordiant, Stephen Kelly, "This capability gives organizations the flexibility to change business processes in a matter of hours, rather than months. The ability to liberate business processes, business policies and legacy data provides a unique opportunity to deliver business value and to realize substantial reductions in operational costs, increased retention rates and selling opportunities."

Howard Smith elaborates, "BPM takes change off the critical path of innovation by creating a new contract between business and IT. Instead of asking IT to implement specific processes, the business contracts with IT to provide a BPM service, extending process design, deployment, execution, monitoring and optimization tools directly to business users. As companies once digitized critical business data using database management systems, companies are now digitizing critical processes using business process management systems. This is the New IT that GE has dubbed 'digitization, a revolution representing the greatest growth opportunity the company has ever seen.' The digitized processes and their management systems become the new platform upon which the real-time enterprise is built, as ERP systems were built atop enterprise data models and databases of the last decade. In this environment, companies are linking familiar process mapping tools to powerful process execution systems to create a new form of organizational knowledge—explicit, executable, actionable and adaptable work design. They are encoding best practices gathered from wherever they can find them, inside or outside the company, and mixing them with unique business processes, their distinguishing ways of doing business. The objective is organizational learning translated directly to operational innovation." In fact, *the learning process is, in and of itself, the ultimate business process.*

Companies want to shift their efforts from further automating individual tasks and move on to managing end-to-end business processes—the very essence of the value proposition of the real-time enterprise.

What Does "Real Time" Actually Mean?

Real time comes in various flavors. If we turn to the definitions proffered at Carnegie-Mellon University, we can see that real-time systems can be classified as hard (catastrophic, dangerous), firm (significant loss of service, annoying) and soft (usefulness, it's late), depending on the implications of not meeting their timing requirements. But, regardless of their classifications, the impact of *time* is key to a working definition of real time:

- "In real-time computing the correctness of the system depends not only on the logical result of the computation but also on the *time* at which the results are produced."[1]
- "A real-time system is universally accepted in the engineering field to be one in which time is a factor in determining the correctness of the result. Usually, this means that some deadline exists which, if the system exceeds this time, it can be considered to have failed."[2]

Furthermore, time is relative to the context of the system. Dr. David Stewart explains, "Real time does not mean fast; it means that a system has timing constraints that must be met to avoid failure. A real-time system is one in which the correctness of the computations not only depends on their logical correctness, but also on the time at which the result is produced. In other words, a late answer is a wrong answer."[3] In most business interactions, real time describes a human rather than a machine sense of time. In an aerial dogfight between military jets, real time better mean real fast, milliseconds to be sure. To the airline passenger whose connecting flight was just cancelled and who is trying to catch the next available flight, it could mean minutes—*in time enough* to make a difference.

In context of the real-time enterprise, our working definition of the real time can be put in everyday terms, *"in time enough to make an effective decision and act, and where a late answer is a wrong answer."* The measure of time depends on the context, and the properties of predictability, fault tolerance and reliability all combine to determine the requirements for the system. Online financial trading will have one set of requirements far different from obtaining online requests for proposals in the construction industry. They have different real-time requirements, but both need information *in time enough* to make effective decisions and act—in time enough to make a difference.

University of Virginia's Dr. John Stankovic enumerated several real-time *misconceptions:*

- Design is ad hoc
- Faster computing hardware will solve real-time problems
- Real-time just means fast
- Real-time programming = assembly language programming
- Guaranteed real-time performance is unattainable

In the world of business and commercial information systems, the term real time cropped up with the advent of the online terminal that replaced the punched card and the batch computer systems they fed. In the early days of business computing, business transactions that resulted from selling something or receiving something into inventory were recorded on paper. The paper forms were put together in batches, and each batch had a control total to ensure that all transactions in a batch were included in data entry for later computer processing. For example, the totals on each order form would be added up to create the batch control total. Once keyed and verified, the batch of transactions was submitted for computer processing. All transactions in the batch were processed at the same time.

The advent of on-line systems and the computer terminal changed the batch transaction processing cycle. Each transaction, not each batch, could be keyed in, validated, and completely processed as a stand-alone activity. To distinguish between the two styles of transaction processing, the term on-line real-time system was used. The results of processing a single transaction were immediately available to all users of the system, all at once, in real time.

The users were, however, clerical back office personnel, and the information delivered to the shop floor, to the sales force, to management or to the warehouse still came in time-delayed paper reports. Although they were fast on-line systems, because time has no impact on the results, even if they were correct, such systems are not real time.

So Simple, Yet So hard

In 2001, Cisco Systems, the company once touted to be the first ever to reach a trillion-dollar market capitalization took a $2,500,000,000 inventory hit. Although Cisco has electronic connections to its suppliers and contract manufactures that made its supply chain so efficient, that it is probably the most documented case study of Internet-driven efficiency, it relied on its customers' purchasing agents to estimate their up-coming requirements for Cisco gear. The purchasing agents of Cisco's customers would place large orders, sufficient to keep up with the exploding dot-com market, knowing they could cancel those orders at any time. They did. Cisco's supply chain worked as it was supposed to, but Cisco's blind spot was its demand chain, and it paid the price for the lack of accurate sensing of *actual* market data in the demand chain.

The business of keeping business information up-to-date and accurate is no small matter. Today, almost every business has its blind spots, and considering that there are about six million firms in America, information-induced waste, write-offs and snafus are staggering.

Something so seemingly simple, yet so powerful, as keeping information accurate and up-to-date, becomes a problem of immense proportions when it's considered that much of the needed information is outside any given organization. Companies are struggling for true breakthroughs now that, for the past ten years, they have reengineered, streamlined and rightsized themselves. They have tinkered with new age Internet initiatives, and, still, they are desperate for actionable information. Solutions won't be found by speeding up computers, for they already operate in speeds measured in teraflops—a trillion floating point operations per second. Solutions won't be found by recording more data into companies' information vaults—vaults already so full, they create information overload.

Considering all the overflowing silos of information scattered throughout most large enterprises, companies certainly have huge quantities of information. Just about every thing they do, day in and day out, is digitally recorded somewhere, and that state of affairs could suggest why the search for *actionable* information is so elusive. Companies don't need tons of historical information locked away in data vaults; they need *live* information—they need breaking *news* in a format they and their computers can understand, and on which their business process management systems can *act* to make course corrections, create demand and set new trends. When information is recorded, it's history. While information is being created, that's when it's really useful, actionable.

Breaking news, events occurring right now, is the stuff of action, the kind of information companies can use to make decisions here and now. Why is there such a dearth of actionable "news" available to companies? It has to do with three factors.

First, today's automated information systems are essentially record keeping devices. They dutifully record the transactions of the business *after* the events that triggered those transactions have happened. The haggling salesman closing the sale with a customer is the event; the order entry system later records the transaction of the event. Sometimes those events are recorded directly into computer systems. In other cases, they may be recorded on paper, faxed and collected into batches so they can be cross checked for accuracy, then entered into the computer system. A large enterprise has hundreds of computer systems scattered throughout its many divisions and lines-of-business. In conglomerates such as GE, lines-of-business operate autonomously, as though they were independent businesses: GE Capital, GE Aerospace, GE Plastics and so on. Each line-of-business operates with its own set of policies and procedures regarding its business processes and their underlying information systems. Typical of such autonomous organizations, there is often little or no synchronization of information across all lines-of-business. Each sets its own policies concerning when events in the business are recorded as transactions and stored in the many information vaults it controls.

Second, the autonomy of the many lines-of-business and their divisions has resulted in situations where the information they process and control only flows through their own islands. The manufacturing division is custodian of product and work-in-progress inventory information; operations maintains finished goods inventory records; the sales organization custodians customer information and marketing tracks and records market and economic trends and activities. Oh, what a story this disparate information could tell, if it was consolidated, aggregated and synchronized—if it was always up-to-date and made available anywhere, anytime to those who can act on the news it would reveal. No doubt, companies could predict and shape markets, as well as spot bottlenecks, redundancies and other sources of needless costs.

Unlocking information, and business processes stowed away in silos scattered throughout the enterprise, is a right step in the search for new productivity, but only a first step. The second step is to bring together all the islands of information, all the information precincts, so that a complete, accurate and balanced picture is rendered. For that to happen, the picture will be distorted unless the information is current and synchronized across all relevant organizations and systems. Since the information is housed in disparate computer systems that are in and of themselves incompatible, not to mention the incompatibility of their data formats and meaning, the search for actionable information becomes increasingly arduous. But that's not all. Even if actionable information can be obtained, companies then must ask, "Is it financially feasible to act? Is it feasible to 'recompile' existing monolithic systems to implement new business processes, regardless of how vital they may be?" With current technology, analysts have run the numbers, and the answer is "no."

Third, as Peter Drucker explained, the notion of "a company" is, economically, fiction. No company is an island unto itself. It cannot exist or operate without those vital parts that do not show up on the organization chart—its suppliers trading partners and customers. What about *their* islands of information that are parts of the complete picture of actionable news? Cisco could have acted much faster if it had a complete picture of its customer channels as the demand for Internet routers fell, when the dot-com bubble burst.

These three challenges, *unlocking information* in disparate application silos, *synchronizing the currency of information* across multiple sources, and providing *360 degree visibility* across the entire value chain, are the keys to obtaining actionable information—these are the challenges taken head-on by the real-time, process-managed enterprise.

The *Real* Real-Time Enterprise Defined

"Any company, old or new, that does not see this technology as important as breathing could be on its last breath."—*Jack Welch*[4]

Cutting to the chase, *the real-time enterprise automates all those work processes it can, and provides computer-assistance for the collaborative, human-to-human work of the firm, mirroring the way work actually gets done in the real world outside of computer systems. The real-time enterprise embraces not just automation, and not just human-to-human work; it embraces both, fusing human and machine activities into complete business processes that deliver value to customers.*

The real-time enterprise is a customer-driven organization that executes and adapts its mission-critical business processes using a sense and respond infrastructure that spans people, companies and computers to provide information that is timely enough to make effective decisions and act, and where a late answer is a wrong answer.

The real-time enterprise represents a management strategy, not a new killer-app technology. Companies already have most of the technology they need; it's how they exploit that technology that counts. That's where the breakthrough business process management systems come in. Business process management systems enable a company to compete on time without the previously painful and expensive need to restructure or real-locate resources, using heavy-lifting techniques such as mergers, acquisitions or other forms of restructuring.

From the Foreword of this book, Dr. Max More elaborates, "The ideal vision of the RTE is one of companies where information moves without hindrance, processes are continuously monitored and trigger rapid reactions, usually automated according to embedded business rules. RTEs also sense shifts in tastes and practices and respond by offering new products and services. Automated processes easily traverse corporate boundaries, time zones, media and systems. Batch processes and manual input are minimized by ensuring that real-time information among employees, customers, partners and suppliers is current and coherent."

While the past decade was focused on automating inward-facing business processes of the back office (typically 40% of a company's activity), the real-time enterprise automates the other 60% of the business, the outward-facing, human-centered business processes that companies use to interact and conduct business with the outside world. These outward-facing processes are the business-critical operational activities of the firm—they *are* the business, not the after-the-fact record keeping activities of the back office.

The real-time enterprise eliminates labor-intensive manual work wherever possible, yet that is only a sub-goal. The major goal is to assist people, both employees and customers, by providing the new breed of BPM systems needed to *act* on that information to make their work more efficient and effective. These BPM systems provide zero-latency, actionable information by synchronizing processes and data contained in disparate computer applications across the value chain. These value chains exhibit natural, biological behavior as the many participants work autonomously, in parallel, under their own control—starting, stopping; participants dropping in and out—yet, by sharing actionable information, they work together to manage end-to-end processes that deliver value to customers.

Today, it's not a single company that delivers goods and services to customers; it's the multi-company value chain, the overall value-delivery system. Business process management provides the overarching philosophy, the guiding principles for managing such value-delivery systems—the capability to discover, design, deploy, execute, interact with, operate, optimize and analyze complex, long-lived, multi-company, business processes, and to do it at the level of business design, not technical implementation. Connections and information synchronization are driven to the point of unity, for it's not just about the speed of a single transaction; it's just as much about companies being able to make major course corrections, in a cost-effective manner, in days or weeks instead of months or years.

Consider the dramatic restructuring and course corrections the airline companies had to make in response to the events of September 11, 2001. That kind of change didn't mean speeding up reservations systems; it meant rapid structural adjustments and asset redeployments, along with restructuring operations to reflect a dramatic shift in the rules of the game in the industry.

The real-time enterprise uses process-oriented architecture to leverage business assets trapped in existing computer applications to create new or improved business processes, yielding optimal business results with minimal business risk. That means not replacing what you already have with some new enterprise software package, but leveraging your existing assets by combining and recombining the pieces into new means of business process innovation and Operational Transformation. In short, the process-centric approach orchestrates and amplifies existing human and IT assets a company already has, to bring new value to the business.

From risk management perspectives, the real-time enterprise is a breeze when compared to the big-bang, all or nothing technology transitions of the past. The real-time enterprise deploys an automated business-process platform for launching an *incremental revolution*—one innovative business process at a time. Now is the time for a company that wants to dominate its industry to begin the journey to becoming a real-time enterprise.

References.

[1] David Wettergreen, "Introduction to Real-Time Software and Systems," School of Computer Science, Carnegie Mellon University, Lecture 2 - Characterizing Real-Time Software and Systems, 2002.

[2] Theodore F. Marz and Daniel Plakosh, "Real-Time Systems: Engineering Lessons Learned from Independent Technical Assessments," Carnegie Mellon University, Software Engineering Institute, June 2001.

[3] Dr. David B. Stewart, "Introduction to Real Time," *Embedded.com*, January 11, 2001. http://www.embedded.com/story/OEG20011016S0120

[4] Marketspaces, by Jeffrey F. Rayport

Five

Making Profits Out of Thin Air

KEY POINTS: *Why is it that, given two companies with approximately the same capital assets and same number of skilled employees, they achieve completely different results? One struggles, the other grows profits. From where do those profits come?*

In 1630, Jean Baptista van Helmont took an earthen pot and in it placed 200 pounds of earth, and in the earth planted a shoot of willow weighing five pounds. He watered the willow for the next five years, and then removed the tree. The tree weighed in at approximately 169 pounds. The soil weighed in at the same 200 pounds, less about 2 ounces.

Where did the 169 pounds of willow tree come from? Clue: van Helmont's conclusion that it had arisen from water alone is wrong. Give up? The correct answer is that it came out of thin air—believe it or not. Oregon State University forest and soils expert Phillip Sollins explains, "Most of a tree's weight comes not from the water but from the carbon of carbon dioxide, right out of thin air." It is the invisible "P" of *photosynthesis* that pulls carbon out of the air and packs it into a solid substance, cellulose. So when you see a tree, you can think of it as one part water and three parts air, with a sprinkling of soil nutrients.

Fast forward to today's business world. Plant a bunch of people (employees, stockholders, management) in a business with, let's say, $100 million in fixed assets, pay their salaries for the next five years, and then weigh their profits. Assuming a healthy company, where did all those profits come from? Again, the answer is that it came out of thin air. It is the invisible "P" of *process* that pulls the day-to-day activities of the business out of the air and packs them into a solid substance, profits. So when you see a mighty company that others envy, you can think of it as one part strategy and three parts *business process*.

In the work of Joseph Juran, Edwards Demming and other pioneers in the quality movement that transformed Japan into an industrial might, their stock in trade was the invisible "P" in achieving quality in making things. To them, that invisible element, *process*, could be codified, measured and improved, creating quality out of thin air—no new factories or expensive equipment needed. To them, whatever the product may be, the process is the product. Their intangible notions are repeatable, and today we have globalized blue-collar work with quality-certified manufacturing scattered around the world, from Brasilia to Shanghai.

But the story of the invisible "P" is just beginning to unfold as we are now witnessing one of the greatest shifts in the history of business and commerce, the globalization of white-collar work and information workers. Again, that invisible element, *process*, is being codified, measured and improved, creating new profits out of thin air.

The ability to manage real-time business processes, across companies, across the globe, has led to a new business phenomenon, the real-time enterprise. The real-time enterprise squeezes out administrative costs between trading partners. It senses and responds to information outside the firm, that allows for unprecedented business agility that enables it to seize the moment when new opportunities appear or respond to competitive threats. Unlocking information previously hidden in the white space, in the gaps, between participants in end-to-end value chains opens new frontiers in the endless pursuit of new sources of competitive advantage.

We are in the midst of a business transformation, where no job or business process, from the board room to the mail room, will go untouched—from core business processes that embody the intellectual property of the company, to support processes that can be a significant drain on resources if broken or anemic. Deep structural change is being made possible by a new category of enterprise software, *systems-of-process*, that deploys zero-latency Internet technologies to enable business process execution in real time. Equally, if not even more important, breakthrough business process management systems make it possible to *change* those processes, sometimes on the fly, to win strategic and tactical competitive battles as they arise. Companies have always competed on the four "Ps" (product, price, place and promotion) of marketing strategy, but now they must also compete on *time*, and it's the new breed of BPM systems that unleashes time-based competition.

In non-technical terms, a *system-of-process* is a form of automation that is designed for, and totally focused on, the end-to-end business process, as opposed to function-specific automation typical of today's IT systems (such as order entry, inventory management and so on).

While the business person couldn't care less about the technologies themselves, they should care very much about what they can do for their business. They can stamp out information latency (time lags) to bring about Alan Greenspan's notion of visibility across the entire value chain—and systems-of-process can *act* on that real-time information by spontaneously triggering the appropriate business processes, alerting either systems or people to respond to significant business events.

The goals of business process management aren't new—the

idea has been in the air since the beginning of management theory. Long-time business process management practitioner, Roger Burlton, president of the Process Renewal Group, explains, "Over a decade ago the words 'Business Process' came into vogue. Since then, these two innocuous words have been conjoined with a multitude of partner words from 'Reengineering' in the early days to 'Automation' in the latter ones. Some have come and gone, sometimes just morphing into a slightly different moniker. However, the words 'Business Process' have prevailed and are more alive than ever."

"Today, with the addition of the term 'Management' we now can recognize a bona-fide new fundamental that incorporates planning, designing, building, operating, maintaining and improving the business processes and their enabling capabilities forever and for everyone. Business processes are capabilities just as important as facilities, people and technology and, like all assets, must be managed from inception to retirement. Only organizations with effective, efficient and reliable start-to-end processes will be versatile enough to do more with what they have, and adaptable enough to deliver real change in real time."[1]

Every modern management theory—from Total Quality Management to reengineering to Six Sigma, has stressed the significance of the business process and its management. As Burlton mentioned, the most recent emphasis on business processes was prompted in the early 1990s, when American industries were feeling great pain as they found themselves competing against Japan's low cost, high quality products. But, during the reengineering wave of the 1990s, management concepts and theories offered no *path to execution*. In today's highly technology-dependent businesses, that's precisely where real-time BPM now kicks in.

What's new is that BPM software, for the first time ever,

makes it possible for business people to take control of their business processes themselves, by giving them simple, direct manipulation of those processes without the need for intervention from IT. This breakthrough takes long IT software development projects off the critical path of business change, and will accelerate the globalization of business, as well as the localization of competitive advantage.

Commenting on his book, *Business Process Management: The Third Wave,* Howard Smith elaborates, "BPM achieves two critical outcomes. First, BPM unifies disparate management disciplines such as Six Sigma, ERP, Supply Chain, TQM, Lean Thinking, CRM, Balanced Scorecard and many others, into a single discipline that supports both operational innovation, and continuous process improvement. It does this by focusing on the whole process as the center of attention in all methods and systems. This approach eradicates what Michael Hammer refers to as the 'confusion, competition, conflict and cynicism' that arise from the pursuit of multiple simultaneous management initiatives. Second, BPM enables the management of end-to-end work, permitting a meaningful and cost effective focus on outcomes of significance to customers and partners. Isolated or functional approaches to operational innovation do little of long-term significance, for the enterprise is more than the sum of its parts. The 80/20 rule for processes is: focus BPM efforts at the 20% of processes that yield 80% of benefits."

It's not enough to simply deploy a new or improved process to tip competitive advantage in favor of a company. Each competitive process innovation must bend and flex throughout its lifetime, as copycat competitors are never far behind innovating companies. It's not time to celebrate when your company introduces an innovation in your industry; it's time to start running hard. It's therefore certain that strategically important business processes must *change* in response to real-time operational information.

There are many tactical reasons why business processes must change, sometimes immediately, after they have been put into operation. In a long-lived process, a participant may fail to carry out a task. Other participants may drop out all together. The requirements that the process is meant to satisfy may change in midcourse—Juran's Pareto principle teaches that 80% of the effort involves the 20% exceptions of a given process. Further, recognizing that business processes are essentially human phenomena, people-intensive processes are the most critical, for it is people who are most adept at handling exceptions to make processes work. It's therefore essential that BPM systems do far more than support automated transactions; they must support unstructured and semi-structured collaborations among people. Companies have little problem handling the normal interactions of the business, but it's the exceptions that consume time and resources—and eat away at the bottom line with a voracious appetite. That's where the *management* part of BPM kicks in to provide powerful change capabilities in the hands of people responsible for getting work done.

For example, if a truck traveling from Mexico to deliver just-in-time monitors to Dell Computer in Round Rock, Texas, goes into a ditch, the real-time BPM system notices the process disruption and notifies people and automated systems of the event, perhaps suggesting corrective action. Without having to go back through a traditional IT software development cycle, a new participant, let's say a warehouse in California with comparable monitors, can be plugged into the process, including the logistics sub-processes unique to that warehouse, on the fly. Exception handled; end-to-end business process continues; time and money saved—and, most important, customers are happy.

In much the same way the Japanese optimized quality to gain manufacturing dominance in the 1980s; companies that embrace BPM will cut their administrative and operational costs by as much as 50%, while, at the same time, create innovative business processes to go after market opportunities with previously unimaginable speed and agility. Real-time BPM is changing the very face of competition across every industry as companies learn to compete not only on products or price, but also on the new competitive variable, *time*.

Systems-of-process are not about some new function-specific enterprise software packages; they are about a shift in a company's business architecture that can exploit the business and IT assets you already have in place. This means not having to tear apart your company to painfully *convert* to some new monolithic software package, enterprise system or killer app. Instead of disruptive change, BPM means an incremental approach to change that is in concert with the strategic goals of your organization, and in step with the speed of your business.

Some of the most powerful forces at work in our lives today cannot be seen. Just count the number of gadgets in the room you are sitting in right now. Those gadgets are driven by the invisible power of electro-magnetic energy. Like those who practiced the teachings of Juran to create quality out of thin air, companies that understand the business-process revolution are forging new value-delivery systems to dominate their industries.

They are creating profits out of thin air.

"It's Not the Economy, Stupid"

"It's the economy, stupid!" was the Clinton-Gore campaign slogan in 1992, aimed at George Bush, Sr. Although Bush had a significant approval rating for liberating Kuwait with Desert

Storm, there was a mild recession because of the transition from a "Cold War" economy to a peacetime economy. Clinton-Gore swept the election and enjoyed six or so years of the "peace dividend" from Ronald Reagan's and George Bush's bloodless victory over the Soviet Union. Pundits say Clinton-Gore claimed credit for a strong economy they had no hand in creating—not to mention Al Gore's supposed "invention of the Internet."

Like politics, business isn't always fair, and the reversal of fortunes can leave former winners stunned and bewildered. This is the case today for many companies, since the roaring Nineties came to a close with a bang—the dot-com crash, the events of September 11, corporate scandals, and the implosion of public markets. Business is hard, and from time to time gloom fills the air of the business world like a choking smog. During such times, business people often blame the downturn in company performance on "the economy." Yet the perennial business *excuse*, "it's the economy," is a flimsy excuse, at best.

Achieving sustainable competitive advantage in business has never been so difficult—business isn't glamorous or easy; it's difficult, often very difficult, *work*. Indeed, it is the way companies organize and accomplish work that is the secret to success, in good times and bad. That's where BPM comes in, as it provides the foundation for cutting costs in a downturn, and propelling growth in an expanding economy.

In a world where companies are increasingly looking to save money by leveraging existing assets, *real-time* systems-of-process present a smart and timely approach to tackling both IT and business challenges. The Aberdeen Group confirms the importance of process management. "BPM gives organizations the ability to cut operational costs at a time when the economic downturn makes it increasingly difficult to boost revenues.

Business Process Management enables government agencies to dismantle obsolete bureaucratic divisions by cutting the labor- and paper-intensive inefficiency from manual, back-end processes. Faster and auditable processes allow employees to do more in less time, reducing paper use as well as administrative overhead and resources."

In a downturn, companies must focus on *execution*. They cannot afford to implement the latest fashionable management theories, new organizational structures, or esoteric new computer applications, especially not on the basis of dubious or tentative return-on-investment. Companies can use process automation to reduce human involvement if required, but they should recognize that its role is far more significant than mere automation. Processes can amplify the productivity of employees, and improve the quality of their work.

By contrast, in an upturn, business process management is just what companies need to accelerate innovation ahead of competitors. It doesn't seem to matter if we are in an upturn or a downturn; the demand for process improvement will be eve rising and will change the "economics of the economy."

If Clinton and Gore were process smart and were running for the White House in 2004, their campaign slogan would no doubt be, "It's the process, stupid!" Quit hanging around waiting for the economy to turn around. Take control of your business processes today and succeed in any economy!

References.

---

[1] http://www.dci.com/events/bpm

Six

The Globalization of White-Collar Work

KEY POINTS: *Real-time business processes have made it possible to go far beyond the globalization of blue-collar work, and on to one of the greatest business transformations of all time, the globalization of white-collar work. Business process outsourcing and off shoring is a mega trend that will affect almost every company in almost every industry. In lieu of growth markets, and faced with growing uncertainty and global competition, the off shoring of white-collar work, for better or for worse, continues at a relentless pace in pursuit of Operational Transformation.*

From customer service to back office record keeping to R&D, the new ability to interconnect business processes digitally, in real time, has allowed Global 2000 firms to go to the ends of the Earth to find certified, high quality and low cost labor. As a result, the locus of economic power can be seen shifting from the Atlantic to the Pacific—from New York, London and Frankfurt; to Shanghai, Bangalore and Beijing.

That last phone call you made to a customer service representative to straighten out your book order from Amazon.com or that call a GE Aerospace engineer made to get the superseded part number on a jet engine could have, as well as not, been handled in Bangalore, India, by a customer representative speaking in a Midwest voice easily mistaken for Johnny Carson. In either case, the customer representative is able to meet the unique demands of the customer by triggering new, existing or tweaked business processes, right there in real-time. These processes may involve diverse participants and activities: an order submitted to a warehouse in Kentucky, a credit check with a London bank, or a call tag request for a UPS pickup in Munich. Further, all these coordinated activities are needed to handle exceptions to a larger business process that is waiting on the completion of one or more of the activities. BPM systems' rapid response to the changing state of live business processes can indeed go directly to the bottom line, eliminating costly, time-consuming and labor-intensive faxes, phone calls and the like..

Whereas blue-collar workers work with things; white-collar workers work with symbols, with information and knowledge. Just as circumstances were ripe for globalizing manufacturing forty years ago, creating a rust belt in America's Northeast, the Internet has created a circumstance for a massive transformation of white-collar work. Today, "Made in America" or "Made in Japan" are less relevant as most goods are "Made Everywhere" with components built just about anywhere (although the lion's share goes to China with its rock-bottom labor rates). Location has become a big blur.

The same is now happening with white-collar, professional jobs, and portends a massive restructuring of the economy and what it means to be a company. We are witnessing the greatest professional employment migration in history. We have now crossed the globalization threshold for knowledge-based work, and the implications for business strategies are enormous, as companies unbundle and rebundle themselves into stateless, transnational enterprises.

Transnationals will seek out low-cost labor in every aspect of their operations as they search for both cost savings and quality improvements (73 million people work for multinational companies worldwide). Indeed, globalization is a very real phenomenon, and is transforming the world economic system, including not just production and distribution, but all aspects of business. Globalization is the central organizing principle of the post-cold war world, and the Internet's ability to carry real-time business processes through its pipes makes it possible to shift knowledge work, as well as manufacturing, across the globe.

It's common knowledge that much of the Redmond software (Microsoft) that we all use is partially developed and supported in Bangalore, India. Software development is an obvious example of white-collar globalization. But some will counter that only the *low-level* knowledge tasks of coding are translocated to India, while the high-level creative design is still on the West Coast. Don't be fooled. Many Indian software companies are ISO certified and climbing Carnegie-Mellon's Capability Maturity Model (CMM) ladder, where reaching CMM Level 5 means only a paradigm shift can lead to further process improvements. Innovation knows no geographic boundaries.

So where do innovation and paradigm shifts really come from? One answer lies in the notion of *clusters*. Silicon Valley innovation isn't restricted to the research labs of the big companies or the famous universities located there. The Valley innovates to the extent it does because there is a cluster of technologists who live in the same area and frequent the same bars. As international software development clusters climb the quality ladder in the way that Japan did in manufacturing, the likelihood of paradigm shifts increases astronomically. Innovation becomes stateless, and even the most creative, most esteemed jobs migrate to clusters of excellence around the globe (90% of Hollywood's animation production happens in Asia). In 2004, China began speaking of technological nationalism, meaning that the country wants to create autochthonous technologies and standards, making innovation an indigenous national asset, not an import.

The lesson here is that it's not just the corporation's low-level, low-wage jobs that are being globalized. Finance and accounting services for GE Capital are managed worldwide from India. Basic research is booming in Russia. Here are some indicators from India: American Express processes internal financial transactions for all of Asia and employs 600 people, while the U.S. finance organization has shrunk by 60%. GE Capital employs 2,000 Indian people managing global payroll, call centers, and mortgage and insurance claims, and was expected to have 8,000 by the end of 2003. British Airways employs 750 Indian people to handle an array of back office applications.

We've had it drilled into us that e-business requires us to extend our business processes and knowledge bases to our suppliers, customers and trading partners. Looking at Michael Porter's fundamental notions of value chain analysis (buy—add-value—sell), the buy and sell components are fairly well understood and put into practice via e-procurement and e-selling. But what about that centerpiece, *add-value*? It's here that you won't find much analysis in the business literature, but it's also here you'll find the next frontier.

Companies shouldn't extend business processes only to their materials suppliers and customers; they should also include strategic business partners. They must zero in on their internal *core competencies*, on the ways in which they add value, as they unbundle and rebundle their organizations in the global economy. It won't be just the satellite/fiber hybrid networks that drive the continued globalization of *highly skilled* knowledge workers, it will be the ability to blend content and knowledge management, including e-learning, and extend it to core-competency partners across the globe. For example, GE has transformed Thomas

Edison's 100-year-old research labs in Schenectady, New York, into GE Global Research, relocating many research activities to Shanghai, China, and Bangalore, India. By the way, 100 years later, GE labs are still reinventing the light bulb. "GE Global Research announced a major breakthrough in a new lighting technology based on Organic Light-Emitting Diodes (OLEDs) that has the potential to be more energy efficient and revolutionize lighting design, while producing the same high quality white light as traditional light sources."[1]

We have crossed the threshold to the globalization of innovation itself. The search for intellectual and capital resources extends to the very heart of competitive advantage, innovation. For example, after World War II, Japan was the source of cheap labor, full stop. In 2004, the Ford Motor Company licensed Toyota's innovative hybrid automobile technology, assuring Toyota a place of dominance in the industry for years to come. Detroit and Silicon Valley, for that matter, no longer have a monopoly on innovation.

Nor does Boeing design and make planes just in Seattle any longer. Boeing provides a world-class example of online process collaboration. Boeing designed its 777 in cyberspace by electronically sharing design tools and processes with engineers, customers, maintenance people, project managers and component suppliers *across the globe*—no physical model; no paper blueprints. The result is that "The 777 is a bunch of parts flying together in close formation." Consequently, Boeing's customers no longer have to wait three years for a plane, for Boeing now aims to deliver a plane in eight to twelve months. Boeing taps global resources to become a time-based competitor.

For better or worse, we have already crossed the threshold to the globalization of our most prized asset, the *value-adding core competencies* of our enterprise. Companies are in pursuit of finding the right people and resources, wherever they are, to optimize their performance. The global village is now a global workplace, thanks to the connectivity of the Internet and the unfolding ability of companies to tap that connectivity for business process innovation.

Historians will likely measure the scale and impact of white-collar globalization against the Industrial Revolution itself. Fat cats sitting in the plush headquarters of American companies—beware. A fully qualified and certified, $30k a year CxO in Durban, South Africa has her eyes on your $250k job, and wants a virtual seat in your real-time enterprise.

The Internet is not about a Web site; it's about the transformation of the global economy. And, by the way, *Caveat India.* The combination of BPM software and next-generation self-service systems are likely to recast two of India's growth industries as sunset industries. BPM software will drastically reduce the need for labor-intensive software development for business process implementation and change, and advanced self-service systems will drastically cut the need for customer service representatives, as growing numbers of customers serve themselves in real time.

References.

---

[1] http://www.ge.com/stories/en/13133.html

Seven

From Science Fiction to Ubiquitous Computing

KEY POINTS: *In the interlocked cycles of technology and business advances, the issues companies face are not just about business, not just about technology. They are inseparably about both. Technology enables, business changes. The notions of the real-time enterprise and business process management can make a business person's eyes glaze over, as the terms are typically seen as just more management theory and, of course, more dot-com Internet hype. Where's the substance? What's really new in technology, especially with regard to the universal connectivity of the Internet, that can enable breakout business transformation? While most business people are comfortable using the term "computer," they should be equally comfortable knowing how XML and Web services provide a foundation for a universal business information system, and enable a new way of competing.*

"Revolutions never go backward."
–Wendell Philips, American abolitionist.

Science fiction films and books paint the picture of how computers will work in the future. The fundamental concept is ubiquitous computing where all the information (data, process and control) is "just there"—and the computer, per se, disappears. The user's perception is simply a rich information source.

Over the last decade, breakthrough Internet technologies have taken us from ubiquitous computing as science fiction to ubiquitous computing as a fact. In the mid-1990s, the Java programming language was the first big step toward ubiquitous computing, by providing a way to shuttle software programs around the Net. In 1998, the eXtensible Markup Language (XML) did the same thing for data. XML provides a flexible way to create common information formats and share both the format and the data on the Internet. XML enables *extensible* data-exchange formats, and gives industries the flexibility to create their *own* data tags to develop a shared Internet file system. Java turns the Internet into a single, ubiquitous computer; XML turns the Internet into a ubiquitous filing cabinet. With Java and XML working together, the result changes science fiction to fact throughout cyberspace. We no longer have just programmable computers; we now have a programmable Internet.

But there is more. As technologists became more comfortable with XML, they developed the idea that function-specific computer applications could be tapped to render selected business process fragments as XML *Web services* that could, in turn, be shared with business partners. Instead of Java moving all about through the Internet, BPM systems could choreograph those business process fragments for higher-level business purposes, end-to-end business processes.

Thus XML has a finger in every pie in the world of ubiquitous computing. Smart companies are working to harness this game-changing technology in ever increasing ways.

The Return of the Business Document

For hundreds of years, businesses have used *documents* as the basis for conducting business. Prior to the computer, documents drove manual business processes, from starting a business transaction to flowing with the transaction until it was complete and stored for future reference. A document was opened, entries made. Purchase orders were edited to reflect inventory availability. Documents passed between trading partners who added or edited their parts of information as they did their piece of the work. They were transformed into picking slips for the warehouse, and transformed again into shipping documents and invoices. Documents are totally natural to business people—they are part of the DNA of a business.

But with the advent of computers, documents were shredded into bits and held in binary electronic forms that bore little resemblance to the original document. At first they were punched into cards and given the artificial constructs of fields, records and files for their storage and retrieval. Later they were keyed directly into online terminals with their renderings being "green screens" shared only among back office clerks. Only the computer applications that manipulated the shredded data could read them, and green-bar reports were the only clues of what lay in the piles of electronic bits held in electronic storage vaults. Where did the oh-so-familiar document that business people understand and use, go?

The significance of using a markup language over a traditional file system or database is that the definitions of data are stored along with the data itself instead of the applications that process the data. When definitions that create and maintain data are bound to the application, only that application can make sense of the raw 1s and 0s actually stored in the computer. Because business information is tagged and readable with XML, there is no guesswork on what a number is or isn't.

With XML's self-describing data, documents can be sent to customers', suppliers' and trading partners' computer applications completely independent of the application that created the data. That is a dramatic breakthrough because it lets businesses communicate electronically in the way they communicate with paper documents where the information shown on a document is accompanied with labels indicating what each element means. *XML is about self-describing digital documents.*

A second feature of XML is that it can describe any kind of information. XML can contain documents, sounds, graphics and motion pictures as easily as rigid text and numbers stored in traditional databases. This allows rich information structures to be defined that can support just about any aspect of doing business, not just numbers and text used in accounting and record keeping. Furthermore, XML preserves the relationships among data elements rather than fragmenting them into meaningless, disjointed tables typical of traditional database systems. Considering that it is the complex relationship of multiple data elements that yield information, *XML is about information, not data.*

A third fundamental characteristic is the "X" in XML. Because XML is *extensible*, elements can be added to a document without affecting existing elements or their use. Because the information contained in XML is parsed, the person or computer program using it simply works with those elements of interest, ignoring the others. This feature of XML provides unprecedented savings since trading partners can add elements specifically of interest to them without affecting current or future trading partners that share a particular type of document. This takes a maintenance burden off of IT, since redesigning traditional database schemas is no longer necessary as change occurs. This also means that the same document can be extended while "in flight," supporting a long-lived business process where multiple companies add information relevant to the process.

The XML digital document, understandable by both humans and machines, allows its users to add new items of information—even to the levels of the "sticky note" addendum. This extensibility capability is needed to meet ever-changing information requirements for exchanging, marking up, and otherwise working with digital documents. *XML is about an extensible information base, not a rigid database.*

A fourth characteristic of XML is its extreme flexibility in rendering information in just about any format. XML documents can be transformed and formatted for a word processing document, a spreadsheet, a Web page, or a screen on a mobile telephone. The exact same XML information base can drive all these media, and the information producer can pick and choose the appropriate elements for the required renderings. *XML is about transformations of information for any format and any device.*

An individual company can define its own document types using XML, but the true value emerges when two or more companies—or better yet, a whole industry—converge on common definitions. Then, companies are able to communicate not only within their walls, but also to others, in clear unambiguous ways. Of course, common definitions are needed, otherwise, XML would create a digital Tower of Babel.

Using the Internet as a communication backbone, the latency of document passing can be removed, and documents can be maintained within the context of end-to-end business processes. With XML, documents can return to their natural forms, free of unnatural structuring for binary storage and retrieval.

The advent of XML means that self-describing, extensible documents can be managed as easily and understandably as the paper records scribbled on faxed documents today. Self-describing XML documents are a digital mirror image of the paper documents already burned into the DNA of business people, so that no matter how different their computer systems are, they can all understand the documents they use to interact with others. The ultimate breakthrough is in the management of digital documents in the context of end-to-end business processes. Indeed, business computing has come full circle; the electronic business document has returned to center stage as the means companies use to communicate with their suppliers and trading partners to meet the needs of never-satisfied customers.

Industry veteran Larry Alston elaborates, "It's outrageously expensive to automate highly dynamic, paper intensive processes that need to integrate with monolithic applications and fixed database definitions. The use of XML for representing these paper documents is crucial for it can support the ability for those documents to change dynamically and cost efficiently. The analogy that has always worked for me is talking about these new services-oriented XML-based applications as the electronic way to automate paper-based processes that touch up against the value chain. There is a ubiquitous flow of paper, and there are in/out baskets, mailrooms, fax machines—where documents are pooled, sequenced, annotated and moved on in the process. That's the way business works."

As a document-centered technology, XML is ideally suited for message passing between trading partners in an e-business ecosystem. Document messaging is a way for e-business applications to interoperate in a loosely coupled, request-for-service, communication process. The document type definition alone can identify a given document type in a business-to-business transaction. But XML wasn't the first attempt at creating digital documents or identifiable document types. For years, large corporations have used electronic data interchange (EDI) technologies. EDI also provides the capability to identify document types. For example, an ANSI X12 EDI 850 is a Purchase Order transaction set. By sending such a document to an EDI enabled system, the receiving organization knows what processing services to perform on the data. Such data hand-offs trigger business processes in the receiving organization based simply on knowing the document type contained in the message sent to it.

Fortune 1000 companies have had EDI and other e-links for years. But these tools for business-to-business activities have required huge IT staffs and all the other assets necessary to operate these expensive and complex systems. They've allowed the giants to gain digital efficiencies with their tier-one and perhaps even their tier-two suppliers and trading partners. But XML over the Internet makes it possible to go much further, including suppliers' suppliers' suppliers, from tiers one, two, three, and so on to tier *n*. Tier *n* might be the Sony component maker in a back alley in Bangkok, or the commodity trader in the Kowloon district of Hong Kong, or the local banker in Tuskegee, Alabama. These are the actors that must be brought onto the value-chain optimization stage. They are certainly not players in today's world of EDI, as shown in 1998 EDIFACT statistics in Figure 7.1.

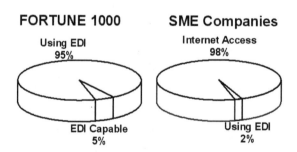

Figure 7.1. EDI Penetration
(Source: David RR Weber and Klaus-Dieter Naujok)

Why is the small-to-medium enterprise (SME) so important? They are the true backbone of the American—and the global—economy, and, as such, they are the backbone of value-chain optimization. According to the Small Business Administration, of the 5.6 million firms in the U.S., a mere 16,378 employ more than 500 workers. Approximately 5.5 million firms employ fewer than 100, while approximately 5 million employ fewer than 20. The next frontier of "Internet automation" is the little guy, who may never use more than a Web browser and a spreadsheet. Smart companies realize that the SMEs are also the weakest links in overall value chains. In terms of value chain business processes, these weak links represent opportunities that can be addressed by bringing EDI-like capabilities to all. For all their expensive EDI technologies in companies such as Wal-Mart, value chain optimization will remain elusive unless they can bring digital dial tone to their suppliers' suppliers.

What's likely to emerge to support even the smallest of businesses will be similar to Internet service providers (ISPs) such as AOL. AMR Research's Executive Vice President, Bruce Richardson, has been tracking the notion of what we call a Business Process Network (BPN), where small businesses subscribe to the BPN just as they now subscribe to an Internet service provider. Just by using simple email and spreadsheets, small companies or individual business people will be able to exchange documents—such as price lists, purchase orders, acknowledgements, advanced shipping notices, invoices, and more. The BPN host provides the needed BPM systems and software. The intent is to automate the transactions and eliminate phone calls, faxes, and the resultant errors that come from manual processes. These BPN users can place an order, sending an XML-encoded spreadsheet via email directly into ERP systems of larger trading partners. When the order is received, an acknowledgement is automatically generated and sent via email back to the small business trading partner. Likewise, shipment notices and invoices are generated and sent via email.

The BPN could become the de facto backbone for collaboration on forecasts and replenishment, trade promotions, product design, and sourcing and procurement. If the BPN model catches on, it could take functionality from supply chain management, product lifecycle management, and sourcing and procurement, and make it available as *a software-as-a-service* offering. The BPN model has compelling benefits. For one, it allows users to work with tools they are already using—email and spreadsheets. Implementations can be as fast as 20 minutes. A second is the community building aspect. For example, a manufacturer can create a trading partner list template to send an email invitation to suppliers inviting them to join its business network by simply clicking on a hyperlink in the email. The BPN community-building services for the manufacturer can include partner network management, partner invitations, publishing new document formats, and other business interaction services. By providing both transactional and collaborative business process management, the BPN is poised to become a foundation for building and strengthening business relationships and trading communities, regardless of a company's size.

From Here to the New Way of Competing

Each stage in the advancement of business technology presents new competitive possibilities, causes irreversible change to the computing environment, and presents business and technology professionals with a new problem-solving paradigm. Each paradigm shift pushes the envelope of what is being automated in the business. At each stage, the challenge for business is to extract competitive advantage from technological breakthroughs. If a company cannot meet each new paradigm challenge, it's at risk from competitors that can.

The future does not suddenly just appear. It's arrived at one step at a time. The last big step was using technology to streamline the back office. The current step that companies must take to remain competitive is to light up the front office work processes and reach out to customers and suppliers digitally. Remembering that the customer is the ultimate goal, companies must not simply become a quick reacting part of their value chains, they must focus on demand creation and set the market, just as Ralph Lauren sets new trends in the fashion market. How do companies command markets? How do they innovate a value chain to, for example, create significant cost advantage?

Peter Drucker explains, "The legal entity, the company, is a reality for shareholders, for creditors, for employees and for tax collectors. But *economically*, it is fiction. What matters in the marketplace is the economic reality, the costs of the entire process, regardless of who owns what. Again and again in business history, an unknown company has come from nowhere and in a few short years has overtaken the established leaders without apparently even breathing hard. The explanation always given is superior strategy, superior technology, superior marketing or lean manufacturing, but in every single case, the newcomer also enjoys a tremendous cost advantage, usually about 30 percent. The reason is always the same: the new company knows and manages the costs of the entire economic [value] chain rather than its costs alone."[1]

Some analysts observe that there are *channel masters*, 800-pound gorillas, in every value chain, such as Wal-Mart or Home Depot, that dictate much of what happens downstream. The reason they are gorillas isn't just a scale thing; it's because they are close to the customer and have the knowledge about what sells, at what price, and what positioning products should have.

GE's Jeff Immelt summed up the challenge in a talk entitled "The Innovation Imperative," delivered at Cornell University in April 2004. "... Some of the biggest transformations in the last decade have been distribution based: Wal-Mart, eBay, Dell.

Given the new power of distribution, the notion of having to sell undifferentiated products is just brutal. Unless you can differentiate yourself, unless you can present yourself to customers, you can't make margins and you can't make money."

While the company closest to the customer has obvious advantage, overall value-chain optimization will be precluded if the lead company hoards demand-chain knowledge. In some cases, hiding customer information is simply not possible. If, let's say, GE and Home Depot cut a deal to sell GE brand major appliances through Home Depot, Home Depot only provides the retail store and the sales transaction, while GE warehouses, finances, delivers, installs and provides warrantee services. In this scenario, there is no way GE won't have upstream customer information—information that drives innovation in trying to satisfy never-satisfied customers. Regardless of your company's position in a value chain, the best way to get close to customers is to boost their productivity, to boost customer care throughout the lifecycle of consumption of the goods and services your company offers to your customers. However, the ability to deliver excellent customer care is only as good as the real-time business processes that drive it with remarkable responsiveness. That's the kind of Operational Transformation that winning companies will make.

Value-chain gorillas can often be lulled by their prowess. In the model described by Drucker, an unknown ran around Borders and Barnes and Noble to create a value chain where there was none—Amazon.com became the new gorilla on the block in the retail bookstore industry.

Amazon.com didn't just create a disruptive new value chain from scratch, it did so by focusing on the needs of the customer, from the outside-in, and by designing everything inside to become a proactive and adaptive demand channel totally driven by its customers. Once the Amazon executive team set the vision, they ran hard and fast to become Earth's largest "everything" store, auction site and marketplace—it's even in the business process outsourcing business, operating Borders Books online. That's value-chain innovation. On the other hand, those who succeed in creating innovative value chains must optimize them over their lives, not just at their initial birth—they must keep running hard.

In 2002 Amazon.com blended its retailing in cyberspace with the advantages of real brick-and-mortar bookstores. It entered into a multi-year agreement with Borders Group Inc. to provide millions of customers with the option of picking up books, music CDs and DVDs at 365 Borders Books and Music stores throughout the U.S. When customers view a product description page, they have the option to complete their order online with delivery from Amazon.com or to see if the item is in stock at their local Borders store. For each item selected, a list of up to five nearby Borders stores is provided, based on the customer's zip code and product availability. Customers who elect the in-store pick up option will receive e-mail confirmation from Borders informing them the item has been successfully picked and reserved in their name for express in-store pick up. Items ordered online for pick up at Borders stores will be sold at the national Borders store price, or local store price, if lower, with applicable local sales tax added. No shipping and handling fees will be charged, and customers have the opportunity to apply any special store discounts or offers on their orders. Sales for items ordered online and picked up in Borders stores are recorded by Borders Group with Amazon.com receiving a commission. Returns on these items are accepted at Borders.

Amazon.com, provides many lessons for companies that want to compete successfully in the 21st century:

- Its technology is fast, able to serve millions of customers in real time, both with compelling, personalized content, and with business transactions that allow customers to act on what they see. In short, the company gains extreme operational advantage from its technology, including delivery of after-sale customer service.

- It's agile enough to enter into partnerships that can take a vision of a new business model that brings compelling value to customers and then actually *execute* on that innovation.

- It's open to coopetition (cooperating with competitors for mutual benefit), especially when customers demand services such as local in-store pickup at their favorite brick-and-mortar store. Its technology allows the company to create new business structures to disrupt existing marketplace structures, and compete strategically with such innovations.

Speed, agility, coopetition and service are the hallmarks of 21st century competition. Such lofty notions, on the other hand, do not "just happen;" they must be technologically enabled.

Execution must follow vision and innovation. So how did Amazon.com rise from its humble beginnings in 1995, using propped up doors as desks, to become a global conglomerate and household name, commanding partnerships with established retail titans? It just could have been technology-enabled speed, agility, coopetition and service.

A down-turned economy makes it even more pressing for companies to remove friction, and streamline their interactions with their customers, suppliers and trading partners. A key goal is to streamline business-to-business interactions across the value chain; thereby reducing both direct and indirect transaction costs, passing the cumulative savings along to customers, while earning healthy margins. This is certainly no trivial challenge, especially since the value chain belongs not to a single company. Technology-enabled value-chain innovation takes the notions of "cheaper, better and faster" to new heights, and creates new, demand-driven, market opportunities. Companies that succeed in such endeavors will dominate their industries.

Value-chain agility, leadership and innovation are vague notions without having a *capability* to execute with great speed and precision. Operational Transformation to achieve value-chain agility is the next giant step in the co-evolution of the business-technology equation. Real-time business process management systems bring about the possibility for companies—and entire value chains—to actually change what they do, rather than just speed up what they already do.

It is the extent to which anyone anywhere can share a universal information system that makes the Internet the most disruptive information technology of the past 50 years. Like GE, companies that "get it" realize that they must build the real-time enterprise—an enterprise that's able to provide actionable information needed at all levels of work, so workers and managers can take informed decisions with up-to-date, internal and external information, and act on those decisions. In short, the real-time enterprise represents a new way of competing, powered by a new kind of information architecture centered squarely on systems-of-process and business process management. Let the value-chain wars begin.

References.

[1] Drucker, Peter F., *Management Challenges of the 21st Century*, HarperCollins, 1999.

Eight

The Many Facets of The Real-Time Enterprise

KEY POINTS: *The real-time enterprise is not one-dimensional. To fully evaluate what it means and what it portends for business, several facets must be explored: the economic concepts of punctuated equilibrium, the essential technology architecture, how complex systems in nature work, real-time business collaborations, strategic agility versus operational efficiency, and anecdotes from pioneering companies that have embraced business process innovation.*

Supply and Demand Equilibrium

The real-time enterprise lives in a space between two digital worlds: a *supply network* on the one side, and *empowered customers* on the other. It connects to those two worlds with *portals* that enable customers and trading partners to conduct business digitally. The real-time information and business processes delivered through those portals are always on, always available, anywhere, anytime. Operating in the "cloud," the real-time enterprise *listens* for events as they occur in both of the worlds of demand and supply. When those events are routine, digital business processes determine appropriate action and send relevant alert messages throughout the business ecosystem.

When events are not routine, as are many business events, people-to-people business processes take corrective action—a capability requiring real-time collaboration facilities. Humans are routinely involved in handling exceptions, costing time and money. The more that exceptions can be handled by humans with automated collaboration support, the less they will cost, and the more effective the humans will be. A shared information base and shared problem-solving tools allow people to make effective decisions in the shortest amount of time, and implement those decisions to override the results produced by existing automated systems. Business process management systems allow a company to override and exploit existing IT systems without being held captive to the rigid business processes ingrained in them.

In the real-time enterprise, corrective action is not limited to individual business processes or the ability to "react" to operational situations. There is a bigger, more strategic, picture that results when companies can see real-time *key performance indicators (KPIs)*. Such KPIs provide the feedback that is needed to sense and respond to market shifts:

- At the operational level, the feedback reveals if the company is doing things right.
- At the strategic level, the feedback reveals if the company is doing the right things.
- At the operational level, speed is measured in reaction time.
- At the strategic level, speed is measured by the time it takes to make a course correction, to set new business directions, and to modify business processes.

In economics lexicon, reacting to or creating exceptions and shifts in market conditions are matters of punctuated equilibrium (the breakthroughs that occur in spurts that punctuate long periods of little change) between supply and demand. The goal is for a company to disrupt a market and tip equilibrium in its favor. Then, as competitors catch up, the disrupter innovates again.

The Double Leverage of Self-Service

Self-service represents one of the most promising new sources of competitive advantage. Through a new generation of process-powered self-service software, the real-time enterprise "puts customers to work" as employees who handle product configuration, order entry and much after-sale support. This is Dell Computer's well-documented business model, where customers become "prosumers," helping to *produce* that which they *consume*.

Dr. Pehong Chen, a pioneer in e-business and founder of BroadVision, explains how a powerful new generation of self-service Web sites can enable the work of two people to be done by one. "Why have a customer call a customer service representative who, in turn, uses his or her computer to solve the customer's problem? Why not empower the customers to solve their own problems? Let customers explore on their own, for they know best what they want. Let customers troubleshoot on their own, for they know best the nature of their problems. A new generation of process-powered self-service provides double leverage by cutting costs and increasing customer satisfaction."

The real-time enterprise also puts its trading partners to work as its own "departments" by integrating their supporting activities into its own central nervous system, just as Amazon put the book wholesaler, Ingram, to work as its initial warehouse and fulfillment "department." The real-time enterprise puts its suppliers to work as virtual warehouses providing real-time inventory information and just-in-time material flow, just as Cisco and Dell have done with their contract manufacturers.

The real-time enterprise puts all its employees to work in the human resources department through self-service technologies, managing their own 401Ks, maintaining their contact information, and updating their dependents' status information.

The real-time enterprise makes its suppliers and customers as smart as it is, and connects them so they can collaborate to solve problems and contribute to the creation and consumption of innovative new products and services.

Technology Architecture for Systems-of-Process

AMR Research provides a useful model companies can apply as they transition to becoming a real-time enterprise. Enterprise Commerce Management is their blueprint, developed to enable their clients to plan, manage and maximize the critical applications, business processes and technologies they need to support employees, customers and suppliers. As shown in Figure 8.1, the blueprint—a conceptual architecture—consists of five layered services: Information Services, Integration Services, Interaction Services, Exchange Services (a portal into the systems-of-process) and Collaboration Services. These services drive the three major categories of systems that will be used to operate tomorrow's corporation:

- *System-of-Record*—a consistent representation of data about products, customers, assets, suppliers, and employees that includes much of the traditional core Enterprise Resource Planning (ERP) functionality supported by the databases of record.

- *System-of-Process*—provides a consistent set of business rules on an aggregated basis while allowing individual business units to implement and manage key business processes. Systems-of-process are supported by data moved forward out of the system-of-record, and aggregated from external sources to provide a federated view of real-time information that spans the end-to-end business process.

- *System-of-Venture*—enables a company to form specific ventures with external constituents and puts information technology at the center of value-producing activities.[1]

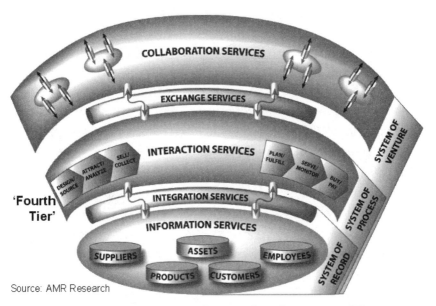

Source: AMR Research

Figure 8.1. From Systems-of-Record to Systems-of-Process

In AMR's model, systems-of-record "record" (store) information about transactions that have taken place. But such after-the-fact record keeping systems are simply not designed to automate the outward-facing, *live operations* of the company. Those operations are the business processes that interact directly with multiple internal departments, suppliers and customers. It is these very business processes that the fully digitized company of the future will automate and manage. And they will not automate them by using existing systems alone; they will automate them with loosely coupled real-time, event-driven systems-of-process, built atop and interoperating with the legacy systems-of-record.

While the systems-of-record will continue to record what *has happened*, the system of process will be what *is happening*, *while also predicting what is about to happen.*

A company's sales and marketing processes, customer service processes, supply-chain processes, logistical processes, procurement processes—every possible business-critical process—will be digitized to provide people with computer assistance in getting their work done.

Yesterday's information systems designs simply won't power the real-time delivery of the systems-of-process. The new way of competing demands a change *in kind* in technology deployed to support systems-of-process. That new category is the business process management system (BPMS).

Large companies must manage hundreds or even thousands of complex business processes that require the information services of perhaps hundreds of legacy applications. As a result, AMR's enterprise commerce management and the real-time enterprise are blueprints for the future. The system-of-process tier in AMR's blueprint is the epicenter, as it provides a home for business process management and the exchange of complete and extensible digital documents. This process tier provides a platform for business process collaboration, first internally, and then across all participants in a value chain, regardless of the systems and technologies each participant uses.

The BPM platform shift occurs at a higher level in the architecture—in what we have dubbed the *"fourth tier"*—that is, above the traditional three-tier IT architecture used in most ERP and other legacy systems of today. The process-centric platform shift is aimed at the ability to deploy business processes across distributed environments, between heterogeneous systems, and across the firewalls of trading partners.

In the system-of-record world, a business interaction simply means committing a transaction to a database. In the distributed and decentralized systems-of-process world, a transaction means the completion of a multi-step business process, such as executing a long-lived business contract.

Looking a little deeper, we can see that digital business transactions, such as retailer-to-consumer, are simple—Browse a catalog and make a selection, then make a payment using a credit card. This kind of transaction is in no way reflective of the complex and nested transactions of real business-to-business commerce or in retail commerce where products or services are customized, for example, ordering a custom computer from Dell or HP. Furthermore, business-to-business transactions in the real business world are often long-lived propositions involving negotiations, commitments, contracts, floating exchange rates, logistics and shipping, tracking, varied payment instruments, exception handling, and termination or satisfaction. Commercial transactions have two phases:

1. Construction—information collection involving catalogues and brokerage systems to locate sources; agreement leading to terms and conditions through negotiation mechanisms; and engagement resulting in the signed contract; and

2. Execution—configuration involving deployment across the group of participants in the transaction; service execution in the context of the higher-level contract and management of exceptions; and termination involving validation and closing the contract across all participants.

Termination may be very long-lived, because contracts may

include ongoing service agreements with online customer service delivery and other aspects of overall customer relationship management. In the world of e-business, traditional transactions are replaced with long-lived, multilevel collaborations.

"In most organizations, the majority of the effort and cost of processing occurs after the initial interaction. Simply automating the front office cannot resolve this problem," said Liz Roche, Vice President, META Group. "Contemporary service organizations require integrated solutions that automate the entire end-to-end process. Managers need to be able to monitor, control and change how work is being undertaken in order to optimize processing and manage to specific business goals."

These capabilities enable the management and change of financial services processes such as multi-product account opening, credit card charge backs, or claim initiation and processing. They also enable businesses to be more responsive to changing economic and business drivers—allowing the faster introduction of new products and programs, being able to respond more quickly to competitive pressures, or providing speedier adherence to new regulations such as the Patriot Act and the Sarbanes-Oxley legislation—by being able to change business processes and policies in days rather than months or years.

In the past, companies have been willing to accept the limitations of monolithic application packages and the expense they create because CIOs felt these applications represented a lower risk for their systems-of-record. They no longer have that luxury and must move to more dynamic IT architectures in order to support more dynamic business process requirements. And they must do this while lowering costs. The process-centered platform gives companies the ability to drive the analysis and development of new business processes, rules and policies, as well as the capability to provide the real-time operational information associated with these processes.

How, in business terms, do companies measure success with the new business process management platforms? A key metric is cycle-time reduction. If companies are successful in providing a zero-latency architecture and straight-through-processing capabilities, then they will see a dramatic decrease in business process cycle times. This is exactly what early adopters already are seeing, while others in their industries are just starting to think about the momentous shift to a process-centric platform.

These observations are supported by Gartner Research who also stresses the importance of zero latency and straight-through processing. They argue that the *information float* problem is the single biggest technical challenge that must be addressed for the successful deployment of distributed architectures. They give the need to address the latency problem a 90% probability, which means that they are almost guaranteeing that companies will make great efforts to solve this problem due to the enormous business benefits.

From Integration to Real-Time Collaboration

While certainly not new terms, *collaboration* and *collaborative commerce* are on the minds of most executives these days—and for good reason. Unfortunately, many business and technical people have sat though more than one meeting where the discussion of the terms jumps straight to instant messaging (IM). Perhaps that's because IM is a hot topic and, for sure, it is one means of collaborating. Sadly, this focus distracts business executives from the fundamental issue. Since they are such common terms, many think they know what they mean in the context of e-business and don't catch wind of what's really going on here. While the typical discussion centers on means of human-to-human communications, collaborative commerce is, at its core, about communication and coordination among human and automated systems to create new value.

In a contributed chapter in the book, *The Death of E and the Birth of the Real New Economy,* Dr. S. P. Rana elaborates, "The most important trends revolve around *collaborative, value-based commerce,* as opposed to antagonistic, transaction-oriented commerce. Even more important, buyers and sellers can now collaborate to create customized offerings that did not previously exist. Through interaction, sellers learn the preferences and priorities of their customers and use that knowledge to create something entirely new—whether it's a portfolio of securities, a customized laptop computer or a complex configuration of office furniture. This enables companies to avoid selling apples against other apple sellers. Rarely will companies be able to take this route alone, however. Complementary suppliers will need to band together—creating powerful partnerships—if they are to deliver high value solutions and avoid being commoditized out of existence."

While early B2C commerce was about transactions, the world of digital business Dr. Rana describes is about long-lived business processes, multi-level collaborations involving multi-party discovery, negotiation, project management, exceptions management, event notification, supply and demand planning, joint product design, workflows, change management and the many other facets of real-world commerce.

Complicating matters even more, each company's *unique* business philosophies and business processes represent its *unique* competitive advantage; and these assets are electronic intellectual property stored in a company's existing information systems. How then can companies retain their individual ways of doing business, yet still participate in innovative new alliances and partnerships characteristic of the new way of competing?

Problematically, the business logic, rules and workflows of companies' internal business processes are "hard-coded" into existing, monolithic applications. To get at this business functionality and enable applications to interoperate is the subject of enterprise application integration (EAI), involving all manner of connectors and adapters. The problem with this tightly-coupled approach is that changing the business processes hard-coded into monolithic applications entails the IT department going in and changing code. Quite frankly, this approach doesn't cut it in dynamic business webs, where the need to create new or improve existing business relationships far outstrips IT's ability to change internal business processes.

Instead of *application integration,* what's needed is a platform to support *process collaboration,* whereby the business functionality coded in a company's applications can participate in dynamic, end-to-end business processes that span the entire value chain. Why integrate at the applications or data levels, when it's possible to collaborate at the business process level? After all, the ultimate target of application integration is the business process, so why not work at that level instead? Why not design and implement business processes naturally and directly? Instead of integrating applications with customers, suppliers and trading partners, why not collaborate with them to execute and manage end-to-end business processes?

Although some dinosaur legacy systems are so brittle that they must be re-architected or rewritten, the secret to successfully creating Web services is to separate out the workflows and business rules from the processing logic of existing applications, and render them as business process components subject to control by a business process management system. In this way, companies can protect the integrity of their existing systems, while gaining the agility they need to dynamically modify work-flows and business rules to form new business relationships.

These new relationships involve companies coming together to form virtual corporations, powered by virtual business processes owned not by one company, but by the value chain itself. Our report on Virgin Mobile USA in Chapter 2 illustrates this scenario. As companies expand their e-business initiatives, business-to-business application integration will become more and more time-consuming and costly. Considering the work, effort and expense of integrating just one cross-company business process, that effort can be multiplied hundreds or thousands of times in a large corporation.

The lesson? Don't *integrate* your computer applications with your customers' and trading partners' applications—instead, *collaborate* at the higher, less technical, business processes level. This doesn't mean that application integration goes away; but it does mean that a company should integrate its existing applications once—and only once—to the business process level, and then collaborate with customers and trading partners at the process level of abstraction. *Integrate once; collaborate at the business process level many times thereafter.* That's the essence of deploying BPM systems, for they provide the command and control of existing IT assets without businesses having to dip into the technical plumbing for each and every business process change.

For the first fifty years of business automation, IT has automated the business. For the next fifty years, BPM systems will be used to automate IT in much the same way that CAD/CAM systems have allowed auto designers to work at the conceptual design level, and the results of their designs are used to automate manufacturing. The auto designer is freed from dealing with the complexity of manufacturing systems in designing an innovative new car. It would take all the programmers in the world to attempt point-to-point integration of the computer applications that companies want to use to manage digital trading relationships, and that's precisely why BPM systems have been developed to support process collaboration.

Dr. Rana elaborates, "Collaboration technologies basically fall into one of two categories: unstructured collaboration (*a.k.a.* information collaboration), which includes document exchange and sharing, shared whiteboards discussion forums instant messaging and email and structured collaboration (*a.k.a.* process collaboration), which involves shared participation in business processes that heretofore have not been automated." Emerging BPM systems support both forms of collaboration, resulting in a powerful new tool for driving Operational Transformation as the next source of competitive advantage.

The Value Chain as a Flock

To understand the true nature of end-to-end value chains, it can be instructive to take a look at what comes after building initial systems-of-process in the fourth tier—and that is the *intelligent* value chain. By looking out to this intelligent era, it becomes clearer how architectural decisions made today can be leveraged as the digital value chain becomes smarter and smarter in the years ahead.

The work of agent technology expert, James Odell, gives a glimpse of what is to come. "Centralizing a corporation was once considered an efficient way to run an enterprise. Decisions and information processing occurred in an orderly, top-down, hierarchical manner. However, it is now clear that this type of system only works in a reasonably stable market. Globalization and changes in technology are causing today's market to be in a state of constant flux. Companies that cannot adapt fast enough to thrive in new markets will be left behind."

"In response, many companies are now building agent-based systems. These systems employ agents that can distribute functionality across a vast computing network. Furthermore, agents cannot only adapt to their environment, but can also evolve by learning from the environment. In short, they are the ultimate in distributed computing. Such an approach prepares enterprises for an increasingly complex marketplace and enables them to respond rapidly to change."

"However, agents and agent-based technology are an evolution, not a revolution. They are being built *from* today's technology and will work together *with* today's technology. While agents, objects, relational databases, legacy systems, imbedded systems, and so on each have their own niche, together they can orchestrate rich systems that none of these technologies could provide alone." Agents must have a network and infrastructure to communicate. The loosely-coupled architecture of the real-time enterprise will provide just such a platform.

Odell elaborates, "Imagine sitting in the park on a nice summer day and a flock of birds sweeps the sky. One moment they are circling, another they dart to the left or drop to the ground. Each move is so beautiful that it appears choreographed. Furthermore, the movements of the flock seems smoother than those of any one bird in the flock."

"Yet, the flock has no high-level controller or even a lead bird. The phenomenon is a result of what is often called *self-organization*. Each bird follows a simple set of rules that it uses to react to birds nearby. When Craig Reynolds of DreamWorks developed his simulation of a flock, each bird behaved according to the following basic rules:

1) Maintain a minimum distance from other objects, including

other birds.

2) Be sociable (i.e., try to match velocities with other birds, if they are nearby, and move towards the perceived center of their group)."

"Orderly flocks emerge from such simple rules. No one bird has a sense of an overall flock. The 'bird in front' is merely a position of a given bird. It just happens to be there—and will be replaced by others in a matter of minutes. The flock is organized without an organizer, coordinated without a coordinator."

"Flocks of birds are not the only things that work like this. Freeway traffic, national and global economies, societies, and immune systems are all examples of patterns that are determined by local component interaction instead of centralized authority. For IT applications this can include order processing, supply chain, shop floor control, inventory management, message routing and management of multiple databases. In other words, a decentralized approach should be considered where local components also have control—instead of limiting your approach solely to the centrally organized one traditionally employed by IT. After all, if New York City can maintain a two-week supply of food with only locally made decisions, why can't a supply chain system perform in a similar manner? Then we would have very robust and adaptable systems indeed."

"Complexity is all around us. Complex systems, however, do not have to be complicated. For example, the ant colony simulation is not complicated. Each autonomous ant has three simple rules:

1. Wander randomly.
2. If food is found, take a piece back to the colony and leave a trail of pheromones, then go back to rule 1.
3. If a pheromone trail is found, then go to rule 2."

"Ant colonies, then, are not complicated. Often, complex systems cannot be fully understood precisely because we do not understand the component interactions. For example, we might be able to identify the components involved in the New York Stock Exchange, yet we cannot accurately predict when we will have a bull market or a bear market, nor when a market bubble will burst. In such situations, our knowledge of the interactions among the various components is not well understood."

Odell challenges companies to ask, "What if we could build IT systems that are as robust and adaptable as those found in nature?" Value chains and markets may not be tangible or legal entities, but they exhibit *emergent behavior* similar to behavior that occurs in nature. By following simple rules and having complete visibility of what other participants are doing, the value chain can shift direction and seek out new opportunities in the marketplace. By gaining greater *visibility of the interactions* of the components in the market, market trends can be better understood, and the individual company can be far more adaptive.

These ideas apply within a company as well. In fact, the whole notion of the corporate hierarchy was developed around the need to move information in an orderly, controlled flow within an organization. But with the Internet and tools like email, orderly flow is no longer the problem—it's making sense of the tiny bits of information that flow horizontally among peers in today's flattened and wired organizations, where everyone has access. Here are some of the first principles that those who see such a future are building into their business and technology architectures today:

- Each participant in the value chain works autonomously, in parallel, but, they are self-organizing, working apart yet together, in synch to achieve a common goal.

- Each participant can see what's going on with its neighbors (and decides which information to share and which to hold private) adjusting business processes more or less depending on the partner, marketplace or customer it is interacting with.

While this future view of the intelligent value chain may seem utopian, its implication is for today: It's the real-time synchronization of the end-to-end business process participants that makes the overall value chain such a powerful market force. With this approach, value chains can be agile and predictive, able to resynchronize in real time as market conditions change.

Lessons From GE

In Peter Drucker's *Age of Discontinuity*, he argues that businesses that want to thrive in the decade ahead have no option but to become, not only more efficient, but more effective and adaptive. It is not enough just to squeeze costs out of the bottom line, for the company with zero costs is not in business.

As the pace of market change accelerates, new demand creation strategies are in order to shape and mold customer preferences the way the food industry does, by innovating new products based on taste. It means creating totally new products to meet unrecognized needs, the way the pioneering banks did when they disrupted the retail banking market by introducing the automated teller machine (ATM). It means disrupting markets by forging new demand channels, even with former competitors when necessary. It means getting so close to the customer that your company becomes predictive instead of reactive as customer needs change.

Despite all the bad and often incomprehensible news that ushered in the 21st century, informed business and technology leaders have not lost the significance of the Internet as a tool to transform business—to create the super-competitive company that can thrive in an uncertain world. With the post-dot-com return of real business fundamentals and reinstatement of earnings as a measure of corporate valuations, businesses are faced with a need to super-charge their productivity, by becoming hyper-efficient and hyper-effective. But how do they go about achieving such Operational Transformation?

To find some answers, let's consider Jeffrey Immelt's rite of passage as GE's new chief executive. *Business Week* reported that, "It has been one of the most tumultuous transitions any new leader has experienced in recent times. The crises began on day two of his tenure when terrorists attacked the World Trade Center. The events of September 11 left him with two employees killed, a $600 million hit to GE's insurance business, an immediate slowdown in its aircraft engine operations, and the prospect of vast uncertainty in an already weak economy."[2]

During the mid-1990s, many companies were concerned that their industries might get "Amazoned"—a dot-com just might turn their industry upside-down. But with the dot-com clutter now cleared away, companies in all industries better be worried about becoming "GE'ed." Immelt's predecessor, GE's legendary CEO, Jack Welch, responded to the dot-com era with his *destroy-your-company-dot-com initiative,* and Immelt has taken the baton and expanded the company's original vision with GE's *Digitization Initiative,* digitizing as many business processes as possible, especially those of the "front room" versus the "back office." GE is intent on making course corrections daily or weekly, rather than monthly or quarterly, saving time and money while better serving its customers.

As the stunning collapse of the dot-coms and the prevailing economic winds led the lemmings among the brick-and-mortar companies to decimate technology budgets, GE increased IT spending by 12 percent to $3 billion. GE "gets it" and fully understands the new real-time battlefront of business. GE saved $1.6 billion from process digitization, roughly 16% of the $10 billion it expects to save annually by 2006. $100 million was freed up by digitizing inventory, accounts payable and receivable processes (operational hyper-efficiency), and a salesperson can handle up to twice as many customers (hyper-effectiveness).

GE's 2003 earnings reached a record of $15.6 billion, with cash flow up 28% to $12.9 billion; and fourth-quarter orders rising 19%. Little wonder the Financial Times once again named GE the World's "Most Respected Company" in 2003, confirming that GE's $10 billion investment in information technology since 1998 is paying off.

As we take a quick glimpse of what is happening at GE, we can see two Operational Transformation themes that apply throughout this book:

1. *Strategic agility*—the ability to restructure the business by changing or strengthening relationships with trading partners and customers, to make course corrections demanded by competitive threats and new market realities. Strategic agility means changing what a company does and how it conducts business, by embracing predictive information systems that can sense and adapt to rapidly changing markets.

2. *Operational efficiency*—the ability to achieve huge efficiency gains, by using computer-assistance for most of a company's interactions and collaborations, not just the routine business transactions. Digital interaction with customers and trading partners can provide up-to-date, correct and actionable information at all times, while reducing the costs, distractions and inaccuracies of conveying information by the usual telephone calls, faxes and paper documents. Prior to the dra-

matic advances enabled by the Internet, such digital collaborations simply weren't feasible. Operational efficiency means doing business with real-time interactions by automating outward-facing business processes that were previously manual activities, and measuring the effectiveness of those processes with techniques such as Six Sigma. The goal is for IT systems to handle the 80% routine interactions of the business, using adaptive business rules to guide their action and trigger events; while people handle the other 20%, the exceptions, as only people can. Operational efficiency requires operating a business that is always open and available to interact and transact.

Peter Lopez, Chief Information Officer of GE Plastics, is on the firing line of GE's total Digitization Initiative and certainly knows a thing or two about setting goals for the decade ahead. When he talks about creating the real-time enterprise he sums it up as a process of *turning on the new, unplugging the old,* a process with three dimensions: digitization, maximizing return-on-investment and delivering digital dial tone.

For Lopez, digitization is about smaller "back rooms" with fewer, more efficient, higher value jobs needed to support, compile and pass information. It's about faster decision making using real-time *digital cockpits* instrumented to display 10-15 critical measures to run the business. It's about increased customer centricity and intimacy gained from better automation of the "front room"—automation of customer-facing, growth driving, manufacturing, selling and controllership processes. In sum, it's about a leaner, faster, more customer-focused enterprise that is far more *predictive* than *reactive,* by eliminating manual touch points, information latency and blind spots.

GE's company-wide Digitization Initiative is not aimed at blindly applying automation everywhere in the organization, but at driving a huge expansion of the front room, so that it will represent 90% of the company's total resources, instead of its current 60%, while reducing back room resources to a mere 10%, down from the current level of 40%. These are the goals made possible by becoming a real-time enterprise and automating those outward-facing business processes used to conduct business with its customers, suppliers and trading partners.

To maximize GE's return-on-investment, functional line-of-business management owns investments in, and benefits from, process digitization. Investments are managed through Six Sigma tollgates that ensure a repeatable approach that puts business processes first and provides visible, stop-go decision points. Metrics are maintained at individual and function levels and provide glaring spotlights to "weed out the old way of doing it." In short, all digitization projects are business-driven projects that are totally visible and accountable, taking senior leadership beyond commitment to full involvement.

This all sounds good so far, but what *digital dial tone* must IT deliver? To reach the desired business ends, information systems investments must be prioritized by business criticalities that focus on business processes in order to determine top information deliverables. Those deliverables include variation-based, outside-in automated monitoring of business processes and proactive alerting, before there is a service issue. This means that IT customer service must be based on service-level agreements, global visibility and escalation capabilities. In short, IT deliverables must be designed and operated for Six Sigma with near-perfect reliability, for GE intends to create the real-time Six Sigma enterprise. GE's Digitization Initiative provides insight into the fundamental assumptions that underlie the need for a real-time enterprise:

- Companies need new sources of productivity in order to

compete. In lieu of growth markets, that means Operational Transformation, based on the universal connectivity of the Internet, to achieve business process innovation.

- New productivity can be found in digitizing operational (front office vs. back office) business processes. New productivity, however, will not just be stumbled upon; its discovery requires thorough value chain analysis both within the enterprise (classical Porter value chain analysis) and outside the enterprise, touching all participants in end-to-end business processes. Because value chains are customer-driven, the analysis must proceed from the outside in—Operational Transformation is all about the demand channel.

- Because operational business processes are complex and cross company boundaries, companies need a business process management capability to orchestrate and monitor dynamic processes that reduce cycle time and increase the overall value delivered to the customer.

- Business process automation requires the supporting services of multiple existing applications that span departments and companies across a given value chain. Marshalling these supporting services requires a new platform for automation aimed specifically at end-to-end business processes—the business process management system.

- Systems-of-process demand real-time information delivery— operational data stores that support extensible, document-like information structures while eliminating latency.

- The real-time enterprise is not an all-or-nothing shift like the monolithic enterprise applications of the past decade. It's about evolving IT architecture, not just applications. It's about loosely-coupled interactions as well as tightly-coupled high-performance transaction systems of the past. It's an incremental revolution, delivering results one critical business process at a time.

These assumptions set the stage for planning Operational Transformation and developing strategies to implement those plans. Although new technologies enable the real-time enterprise, GE's Lopez makes it clear that business strategy is the central issue. On the other hand, he also makes it clear that at GE, technology is everybody's job and is *owned* by the chief executive, not the technology department.

Whether it's a multinational conglomerate such as GE or one of the five million plus small businesses that make up the bulk of the American economy, strategic agility and operational efficiency must be planned for and acted upon. Business agility has never been so vital to the continuing success of a company. Competing for the future demands that companies take the notion of business agility from theory to reality.

The goal is to make information immediately available so that people and computer systems that need it can make informed decisions and act in a timely manner. Such *actionable information* has been the elusive promise of automation since the advent of the electronic digital computer in the 1940s and the early adoption of business computing in the 1950s—until now.

Putting it All Together

Although the form and structure of real-time enterprises vary from industry to industry, they share common characteristics, the first and foremost of which is that of a customer-driven company:

- *Customer-driven.* The supply-push economy, where producers made things and then pushed them to customers, has given way to a demand-pull economy where customers determine what is to be made and when. The customer is no longer king, the customer is now a dictator and companies must respond by changing their business models from "buy-make-sell" to "sell-buy-make"—or else get stuck with unwanted goods and services. The real-time enterprise sells, then buys, then makes—in real time.

- *Agility.* By centering activities on end-to-end business processes and providing information visibility with zero latency, course corrections are possible in real time. The real-time enterprise can detect and adapt to changes in the business ecosystem as they occur. It can take corrective action as and when needed. Because it uses business process management automation, it can create new, or improve existing, business processes in days or weeks, not months or years. It can spontaneously create and personalize business process variants on the fly (yet under policy governance) to meet the unique needs of individual customers, one-to-one. And because it uses advanced simulation techniques to test new or changed business processes, it has confidence that the logic built into those new processes will not diverge, drop into infinite loops or otherwise fail to conclude.

- *Event-driven.* In response to events in the business ecosystem, spontaneous transactions are generated without human initiation and propagate throughout the value chain. The real-time enterprise is an event-driven company.

- *Market-driven.* Because the market owns value chains, companies must not only play their parts as responsive value-chain participants, they must be able to sense changing market conditions and proactively set market trends.

- *Business Process Management.* Because it's the end-to-end, multi-company business process that delivers value to customers, business process management is the focal point, the epicenter, of the real-time enterprise. To refocus on the business process as the central objective of business automation, a new category of software, the business process management system, is essential.

- *Work in Parallel.* Individual companies in a value chain naturally work autonomously, controlling their own work without a central controller. Their work proceeds in parallel—it's loosely coupled. Successful value chains are patterned after nature. The best mimic biological forms, not artificial command and control forms dictated by rigid computer applications. They chatter among themselves, they send signals and they constantly see what others are doing to maintain their position in the value-chain flock—in flight, in real time.

- *Work Asynchronously.* Unlike the serial flow of work in the batch-time enterprise, the real-time enterprise works with other participants in a value chain the way it always has. Things start. They stop. They resume when they can. The real-time enterprise requests services from outside participants, but does not stop its other activities while waiting for a response. It keeps doing what it can to advance its progress towards the goal, all the while listening for that response from others that lets it resume a waiting activity. The real-time enterprise eliminates information float and ensures that all can see the current state of the overall business process. When everyone always knows what's going on, the whole value chain's productivity magically soars, regardless of the many starts and stops along the way.

- *Maximally Digital.* The real-time enterprise strives to be hyper-efficient and hyper-effective by eliminating non-value-adding manual work wherever possible. That means business process automation wherever possible, while creating high-value jobs. The rather simple back office business processes (40% of a company's processes) already have been automated with current systems-of-record. It's the other 60%, the systems-of-process, that represent new sources of productivity and competitive advantage.

- *Collaborative.* The real-time enterprise digitally mirrors the way real business operates. Instead of integrating at the computer application or data levels, the real-time enterprise collaborates at the business process level to conduct its interactions with trading partners and customers. It's not about integrating databases; it's about sending and receiving self-describing messages that trading partners can use and extend without rewiring their information systems.

- *Mediate Demand and Supply Channels.* The real-time enterprise senses and responds to events that occur in both its supply and demand channels, mediating and bringing about punctuated equilibrium in its favor.

- *Always On.* In the global economy, the real-time enterprise follows the sun, greeting the business day in Tokyo, then Bangalore, then London, then New York, then San Francisco—it's always on, 7 x 24 x 365. Customers and trading partners are able to conduct business digitally anytime, anywhere—the real-time enterprise is always open for business.

- *Actionable Information.* The real-time enterprise demands and provides actionable information. That means zero latency so that information is made available *in time enough* to take meaningful decisions—and act on those decisions. It operates on breaking news, not historical information.

- *Operational Data Management.* The real-time enterprise deploys and stores operational data within the business process management systems that need it. A given business process management system receives operational information, executes its unique process fragments, extends the information with new elements, and passes it along to those who need it to complete the work of an end-to-end business process. Real-time information provides the visibility and synchronization needed across the end-to-end value delivery system.

Indeed, the Internet has kind of sneaked up on business, bit by bit, day by day. It's only now that even astute companies have come to fully realize the power of the Internet for Operational Transformation. Companies that "get it" are already well into their journey toward full digitization. Brick and mortar companies like GE with its Digitization Initiative, have been awakened. They have embarked on the journey to streamlining every aspect of their companies using the Net. These companies understand that the Internet was not about the dot-com fad, and they are determined to transform all their operations to dominate the decade ahead through flawless execution.

References.

[1] Enterprise Commerce Management: The Blueprint for the Next Generation of Enterprise Systems, *The Report on Enterprise Management*, AMR Research, June 2001.

[2] http://www.businessweek.com/magazine/content/02_17/b3780001.htm

Nine

The Event-Driven Company

KEY POINTS: *Business process management systems require capabilities, chief of which are event generation and notification services that can provide communication of relevant business events to all interested parties. To achieve such capabilities, corporations can no longer use existing methods such that decisions are tied to cycle times where responses are based on stale information. Instead, they must transform themselves into event-driven companies, where they can sense and quickly respond to changes in information as they happen throughout the business ecosystem.*

The real-time enterprise must be event-driven, where a business event is any significant change in business data or conditions. Event-driven information systems sense and respond to business events: an order is placed, a bank account balance drops to zero, a shipment becomes overdue or a check bounces.

At the heart of an event-driven information system is a framework for event notification to "alert" all interested parties. Alert service capabilities include means to capture and store events, generate new events, and communicate events with little or no delay so that people and computer systems can react to those events in a timely fashion. An alert service framework consists of an event source, an event store or collector, and an alert distributor.

There are several event sources in the enterprise and across the value chain. These need to be identified and enabled to generate the events. Following are a number of examples drawn from various industries:

Data Warehouses. Financial institutions have implemented data warehouses for various business reasons, from customer service to customer analytics. Customer analytics vary from identifying cross-selling opportunities through techniques such as market basket analysis or collaborative filtering, to trend analysis that can flag behavioral patterns leading to defection. The output of the analytics is a rich source of business events for cross selling additional products, or customer care activity to fend off potential attrition.

Customer Touch Points. In an attempt to reign-in operating costs, banks have introduced alternative delivery channels like the automated teller machine (ATM), interactive voice response (IVR) and the Internet to move the transactional interactions away from expensive channels like the branch office. While this might be understandable from the objective of cost control, it reduces human contact that could have served to detect and satisfy a need or address a customer issue. Alerts are well suited to communicate these needs as long as relevant events can be detected. For example, a customer browsing on the bank's Web site for savings or loan products can generate events indicating a potential need. Likewise, a customer verbally requesting a payout quote from a bank service representative at a call center or through touch-tone telephone responses can signal an event flagging a potential attrition. Or, a customer making an address change over the Internet can signal a job change and, hence, the opportunity to solicit a 401K rollover.

Legacy Systems. A majority of large organizations do their core business processing with legacy mainframe applications. These heritage systems form a rich source of business events. The challenge is to unlock the data trapped in these applications to create a new source of business events using various techniques such as Web services technology.

Events take place in the context of business processes that, in turn, are comprised of services provided by computer applications and human interactions. By monitoring business process activities and identifying their completion status or exception conditions a company can trap events that are of significance to the business. In an abstract sense, this involves building a real-time business operating system that wraps around existing legacy applications. In a practical sense, the real-time business operating system is a business process management system, due to its ability to support long-running business processes that run across organizational boundaries. The events generated by the activities of a business process are handled by the alert service framework of the business process management system.

Regardless of the source of events—legacy batch exception reports call center, analytical data warehouses, or Web sites—they are captured and stored in an event data store in the fourth tier, in the business process management system. An alert generator and distributor applies business rules to convert newly stored events to alerts for all interested parties. For example, a bank customer may subscribe to receive an alert when his or her account goes into overdraft. In this case the business rule would transform the overdraft "event" into an overdraft "alert." Even if the customer does not elect to subscribe to this service, an account manager may want to be alerted when the account repeatedly goes into overdraft, in order to prompt selling overdraft protection to the customer. In this case a business rule can be set up to generate the overdraft "alert" when a given number overdraft events occur. This scenario also identifies the need for a personalization capability that allows bank customers to use their personal preference and subscribe only to those events about which they want to be alerted. In addition, the customer can define how the alerts are to be presented: email, a pager, PDA, phone and so on.

Messaging technology is central to delivering alerts or event notifications between two or more computer applications without human intervention. Two characteristics of modern messaging systems reveal why they are crucial to the event-driven company. First, they eliminate any delay between when a business event occurs and alerts are distributed, regardless of the technology platforms used by senders and receivers. Second, they guarantee delivery of a message, even if an intended receiver is not available at the time a message is sent. These two characteristics add up to zero latency and confidence that all event notifications will, indeed, be received by each value chain participant that needs the information for work to proceed.

In essence, messaging technology allows computer applications to communicate in much the same way that email technology enables communication between people. Like email, messaging technology provides for *asynchronous* communications—after an email is sent, the sender does not wait for a reply and, therefore, is not stopped from continuing other work while waiting for a reply. When the reply is received, related work continues at that time.

This method of communication between computer applications is advantageous, as performance of a given business process fragment is not bogged down during peak loads. The process management system does not have to wait for a response from another process fragment, perhaps running in a supplier's system, before continuing other work.

On the other hand, some applications may indeed require a response before they can continue, and, in that case, synchronous communication must also be supported. When asynchronous communications is the obvious choice, either point-to-point or publish and subscribe methods may be deployed, depending on their applicability. Point-to-point messaging involves one sender and one receiver, and is appropriate when a message needs to be acted on once, by the one receiver (for example reserving a seat on a particular airline).

Publish and subscribe systems involve a single sender that publishes or broadcasts a single message to several receivers that have subscribed to particular categories of events in which they have interest. IBM Research explains, "The system ensures the timely delivery of published events to all interested subscribers. In addition to supporting many-to-many communication the primary requirement met by publish and subscribe systems is that producers and consumers of messages are anonymous to each other, so that the number of publishers and subscribers may dynamically change, and individual publishers and subscribers may evolve without disrupting the entire system."

"The earliest publish/subscribe systems were subject-based. In these systems, each message belongs to one of a fixed set of subjects (also known as groups, channels, or topics). Publishers are required to label each message with a subject; consumers subscribe to all the messages within a particular subject. For example a subject-based publish/subscribe system for stock trading may define a group for each stock issue; publishers may post information to the appropriate group, and subscribers may subscribe to information regarding any issue. An emerging alternative to subject-based systems is content-based messaging systems. A significant restriction with subject-based publish/ subscribe is that the selectivity of subscriptions is limited to the predefined subjects. Content-based systems support a number of information spaces, where subscribers may express a "query" against the content of messages published."[1]

In dynamic business-to-business interactions, where participants in a value chain work independently and in parallel, the combination of extensible XML-formatted information and documents plus asynchronous communications with publish and subscribe messaging go hand in hand. When combined with synchronous communications where appropriate, the digital world of the business process management system can mirror how work naturally progresses in the physical world—information is dynamically extended and passed between multiple participants throughout the life of a long-running process.

Complex Event Processing and Business Activity Monitoring

According to Gartner research, event-driven business applications can be sorted into four categories:

1. Simple event-driven (or message-driven) applications where application programs explicitly send and receive messages directly to and from each other.

2. Event-driven applications that are mediated by integration brokers, which transform and route simple event messages according to logical rules.

3. Event-driven applications that are directed by business process management (BPM) engines that manage the end-to-end flow of a multistep process using special, BPM-oriented types of events.

4. Complex event processing (CEP) applications, where a sophisticated event manager logically evaluates multiple events to enable decoupled, parallel, asynchronous processing or business activity monitoring (BAM).

Complex event processing is most effective when event messages carry information relating individual events with other events and causal information on how an event came about. As described in the landmark book on complex event processing, *The Power of Events*, by Stanford professor, David Luckham, some CEP messages may not even carry business data swapped between applications. Instead, they contain information about low-level events that, when aggregated into patterns, can reveal high-level business intelligence. As an everyday example (unfortunately), consider how the intelligence agencies filter low-level noise among terrorist groups to derive meaningful information used to set terrorist alert levels for law enforcement agencies. In a business context, Luckham asserts that low-level events that occur in "the cloud" of network-based business interactions can yield valuable business intelligence. By using complex event processing for business activity monitoring, CEP can close the loop between BAM and the business process management system that, in turn, can act on the business intelligence.

Getting There

Whether it's manufacturing, distribution, retail trades, or services, event-driven systems and the messaging technologies that power them provide the foundation for real-time business process management. Organizations are looking to implement event-driven business process management systems that incorporate powerful business activity monitoring capabilities. To get started, the source of the event-driven alerts can be through animating batch reports from legacy systems and projecting them onto the business process management system. Subsequently, the complex event processing capabilities of the business process management system are needed to generate, capture and analyze even low-level events that can produce actionable business intelligence. Central to the business process management system is its ability to notify all participants—people and applications—so they can respond in real time. By shifting the focus from discrete function-specific applications to end-to-end business process management, the foundation can be established for the real-time, event-driven company of the future.

References.

---

[1] http://www.research.ibm.com/gryphon/Content-based_Publish_Subscrib/content-based_publish_subscrib.html

Ten

Cycle-Time Management

KEY POINTS: *In the past, the only industries that needed real-time network architectures were banking, telecommunications and financial market exchanges. But now that the entire business world is moving to the Net and we are seeing decreases in business cycle times as much as 80%, every company that wants to thrive must become a real-time enterprise. Now there are standards for business processes that finally allow companies to interoperate, share information with zero latency and create rich new sources of competitive advantage.*—Joe Bellini, Bloomberg Interview, London.

Over the years, IT has provided automation support for discrete business functions. Although these business functions (listed on the left of Figure 10.1) are vital, they are not how a company runs its business. What companies want to do is manage their asset-intensive business cycles. They want to manage their purchasing cycle. They want to manage their forecast and planning cycle, the customer service cycle and other business cycles, as illustrated in the figure. Each major business cycle is a complete, end-to-end business process, usually requiring support from more that one company to realize the process.

Cycle-time management is essential to the effectiveness, agility and overall productivity of any company. Reducing information float, increasing information synchronization and achieving near zero information latency are the ingredients of cycle-time management. But there is a problem. The figure clearly illustrates that each major business cycle requires the support services of multiple business functions.

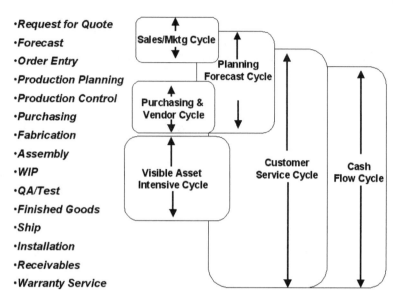

Figure 10.1 Managing Business Cycles

Even worse, as shown in Figure 10.2, the automation of business functions is embodied in multiple computer applications and function-specific software packages: CRM, SCM, ERP, e-procurement and so on. Tapping the business functionality contained in these stovepipe applications, so they can contribute to the management of business cycles, is a huge problem, especially when it is considered that large corporations have hundreds of function-specific applications.

Why do companies spend between thirty and seventy percent of their IT budgets on application integration and maintenance of that integration? It's because they have to, in order to manage these very important business cycles. All they have are function-specific applications that do not support business cycle automation, bringing them to where they are today, spending all kinds of money on an integration infrastructure, and integration projects. Expensive enterprise application integration software is used to create a new business cycle-oriented application by stringing together a group of functionally-oriented applications.

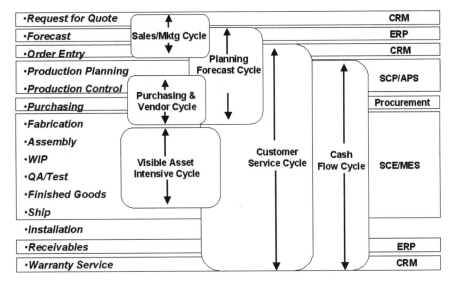

Figure 10.2 Function-Specific Applications

While enterprise resource planning (ERP) packages provide modules to automate and even integrate business functions, their business processes are cast in concrete, after a one-time reengineering initiative. Furthermore, ERP systems are inward focused, primarily streamlining the back office, and bounded by the walls of a single company. Cycle-time management, in contrast, requires business process collaboration with other companies, and that's where current ERP systems hit the wall.

Breaking through company walls by harnessing the Internet, early cross-company applications were developed to go where no ERP system had gone before. After the ERP wave, the next set of process-oriented "killer apps" emerged. For example, the founders of i2 Technologies came out, and said, "The functional application approach is a crazy way to plan out a company's production. It's trying to solve planning problems for each functional department, and then recombine the results into to a production plan."

They asked, "What if I was able to manage the entire visible asset-intensive cycle? What if I could look at demand, material and capacity simultaneously, instead of handling them individually and trying to recombine the problem? I could probably save a lot of money." And sure enough, they went in and they were able to save 70 to 80 percent of the visible inventory by putting out better production plans." i2 broke the established pattern and used a persistent operational database to bring together production data from multiple internal and cross-company applications to solve for the entire supply chain.

Siebel took the same process-driven, full business cycle approach to sales, marketing and customer support under the banner of customer relationship management. Ditto Ariba and Commerce One for e-procurement. They viewed purchasing and vendor management as business cycles, not a collection of discrete business functions. This new wave of applications was made possible by leveraging new Internet technologies and operational data stores, including in-memory databases. Technology enabled these pioneers to innovate with cross-company business process automation. On the other hand, these new breeds of applications were only a step toward a far more encompassing *architectural approach*. As companies gained experience, they learned the value of cross-company packages and wanted much more, for they also learned that it does not make sense to buy yet another, big, monolithic compiled application for business process automation.

Although Siebel, i2, Commerce One and Ariba offer process-centric applications, they, like the ERP packages before them, have their business processes cast in concrete, locked in closed infrastructures. It is very difficult to extract and share data and information from those systems. It is also very difficult to change them, once they've been installed. They cannot flex when the business changes. While they solve a point-in-time problem, they do not provide the architectural elements needed to embrace change. What companies need is an architectural environment that thrives on, rather than crumbles under, change—a process-oriented architecture, not another monolithic computer application. Business process management for cycle time management is not a one-off event; it's an ongoing affair for any business, and change must be built-in.

The more complete the business cycles a company can manage through automation, the faster it will be able to make course corrections, and respond to new market opportunities and threats. Thus the current shift in business automation is not another application shift—the next Killer App—it's a process-oriented architecture, because it provides the capability and flexibility needed to support complete business cycles. To support this thesis, CRM pioneer, Tom Siebel, pronounced that CRM is dead, as he ushered in his company's new cross-application product offerings. In Siebel's vision, "Like most revolutionary ideas, business process software may seem simple on the surface, but it has far reaching consequences. According to Siebel, the CRM market is dead, not because customers no longer need it, but because it will be subsumed within a new layer of software that offers much greater value, just as CRM once subsumed the Sales Force Automation (SFA) and contact center markets. If Siebel's vision is correct, the end of the CRM market also means the end of the Enterprise Relationship Planning market, the Supply Chain and Human Resources markets, and all other current categories of application software."[1]

The different business functions and the function-specific systems that run them will not just go away. There will not be a "big bang," process-centric equivalent of the ERP, CRM or SCM package. The future will be based on a process-centric architecture used to implement the flexible systems-of-process that orchestrate the services extracted from underlying legacy applications. The last thing companies need is another monolithic application dropping into their laps. What they really need is the ability to *incrementally* automate and continuously improve complete business processes that span the value chain—they need agile business process management..

The Internet provides new opportunities for companies to extend their supply chains to their customers, suppliers and trading partners to provide breakthrough capabilities. Traditional supply chain management is being transformed into supply chain event management (SCEM), changing the very principles that underpin supply chain competition. The principles for today's supply chain are:

- Global visibility to information.
- Zero latency whenever possible.
- Synchronization of information flow.
- Ability to manipulate live business processes.
- Optimization of business processes not just within, but also between entities.

Companies are applying event-driven supply-chain frameworks to make the next generation of step-wise improvements in lead-time reduction, elimination of excess inventory buffers and cycle-time improvement. The benefits of executing across the supply chain in a real-time fashion are undeniable, but achieving the benefits requires a unique set of "sense and respond" capabilities to yield results. The ability to collaborate, measure, monitor, notify, simulate and control real-time supply chain events and processes lies at the heart of supply-chain transformation.

Companies are using real-time, process-oriented architectures to accomplish such sought after capabilities as:

- Collaborative demand planning among manufacturers, distributors and retail outlets.
- Collaborative supply planning among contract manufacturers, suppliers and customers.
- Monitoring changes in supply and demand among sales partners, logistics providers, global wholesalers and suppliers.
- Notifying planners and purchasing agents of exceptions in demand and inventory availability.
- Simulating production plans and constraints to validate planning activities.
- Controlling inventory disposition and workflow for strategic sourcing.

The adoption of zero-latency principles and process-oriented architectures has resulted in a new set of dynamics that must be considered in any supply-chain improvement program:

Integrated Demand and Supply Planning. A key to success in creating the real-time supply chain is to integrate demand and supply planning, rather than focusing on each area separately. To do this, companies must change the point in the supply chain at which it allocates goods, while simultaneously altering the point at which they fulfill demand. This can be achieved by shifting the primary focus on the demand chain—the customer.

The demand chain links with the supply chain at two distinct points that can be called the supply-fulfillment point (SFP) and the demand-offering point (DOP). Traditionally the SFP is at the distribution center with finished goods delivery, and the DOP is at the purchasing department of the customer. By moving the SFP further back into the supply chain, perhaps even all the way to manufacturing, and pushing the DOP further up the demand chain of the customer, perhaps even to the point-of-sale, companies can achieve a unique value proposition in serving its customers. Movement of the DOP is the hardest to achieve, and requires personalized process interactions directly with the customer's systems.

Continuous Demand Data. Supply chain organizations must make costly purchasing, distribution and logistics decisions, while dealing with the lack of real-time demand data. Current demand planning processes and applications are failing to predict rapidly fluctuating orders because most of the ERP-SCM applications deliver static pricing independent of market changes. In addition, CRM applications are oblivious to the changes in customer spending patterns that result from price sensitivity and supply chain capacity.

To meet these challenges, demand planners must create market sensitive forecasts directly linked to changing economic indicators, current field-level orders and sales pipelines—not the static data used today. On the supply side, inventory management has to link capacity to changes in demand. Capacity has to shrink or expand, depending on demand, with ever-shorter reaction times. A good example is the airline industry, where revenue management teams decide which flights to cancel and how to price remaining schedules. Revenue management teams can tune their pricing to terms that match supply.

Close the Loop Between Planning and Execution. In the business networks of today, buying patterns fluctuate overnight, making today's optimal demand plan sub-optimal tomorrow. Optimization applications that view supply chain planning and execution as static separate events no longer suffice. What are needed are optimizers that support adaptive planning—a technique that continuously revises a rough plan as actual demand occurs, and operational data is collected. Companies can use an event-driven framework to link customer buying behavior to regional distribution centers, and all the way back to manufacturing centers, providing continuous feedback to close the loop between planning and execution. This is the essence of Collaborative Planning, Forecasting and Replenishment (CPFR), a best practice in supply chain management.

Structured Collaboration. The focus of successful collaboration is not on transactions, but more on time-based events that can be used to gain consensus in the supply chain. Effective supply chain solutions center on sharing time-phased data at set frequencies. Time structured collaborations promise tighter relationships with suppliers, customers and partners that produce more efficient processes and better products. They also can be used internally to unite functional and geographical areas.

Traditional computer applications provide good structure for business interactions, but provide negligible flexibility, while ad-hoc collaborations such as e-mail provide complete flexibility but no structure. What's needed are both ad hoc and structured, process-centric collaborations if supply chains are to be continuously optimized.

Putting It All Together

The fundamental problems of most poorly functioning value chains are caused by the serialization of tasks among participants, combined with a fragmented view of the state of the overall value chain. In short, value-chain participants are stuck in their own swim lanes, and don't have the needed view of the overall end-to-end business process, and its current state at any given point in time. The greatest disconnect can often be found in demand distortion—as witnessed by Cisco when the real demand for routers fell from the sky when the dot-com bubble burst in 2000, and Cisco took a $2.5 billion inventory hit due to blind spots in the demand channel. Providing complete visibility across the entire value chain is the key to superior performance. In lieu of a complete system-wide view of the value chain, synchronizing as many cross-company business processes as possible, to support key business cycles, can also bring substantial improvement. These lessons apply not only to manufacturing, but to distribution and service industries as well.

Appendix B provides a cycle-time management discussion of several industries including:

- Automobile industry and the 12-day car
- Insurance,
- Banking and finance,
- High technology,
- Apparel, and
- Consumer packaged goods.

References.

---

[1] http://www.siebelobserver.com/siebel/trends/vision.htm

Eleven

Thoughts and Strategies for the Real-Time Enterprise

KEY POINTS: *The future is not some destination; it's our own creation. The paths to it are not discovered, they are forged, and the process changes both the path maker and the destination. Building the process-managed real-time enterprise requires changing the mental models of functionally-minded business leaders, business process thinking throughout the organization, and an incremental approach to change. There are no cookie-cutter approaches to Operational Transformation, and companies cannot go out and buy real-time competitive advantage. The real-time enterprise is not a singular change event; it's a way of business.*

In his book, *Systems Architecting,* Eberhardt Rechtin succinctly explained the challenge of business architecture. "Both architects and business managers live in ill-structured, unbounded worlds where analytic rationality is insufficient and optimum solutions are rare. Both have perspectives that are strategic and top-down. Top managers, like chief architects, must architect strategies that will handle the unforeseeable, avoid disaster and produce results satisfactory to multiple clients—to boards of directors, customers, employees and the general public. Their common modus operandi is one of fit, balance and compromise in the overall interest of the system and its purposes."

Architectural thinking allows companies to embrace rather

than cringe at change. *In today's business world, the ability to change is as important than the ability to create, and the velocity of change is only going to increase.* Change may result from new business requirements or the adoption of new business technologies—neither should impede the other.

A process-oriented business architecture is much more than just using process mapping tools. To match the nature of real world business processes, the first principles of process-oriented architecture must revolve around independent, concurrent units of work of process participants, not simple serial flows, and certainly not around functional-management constructs such as organization charts. The architecture must have at its core, the *interactions and collaborations* among those process participants, not just the internal designs of participants' individual work processes.

The business process management system, the engine of process, must have the capability to handle these dynamic collaborations and interactions. That is, the process engine must have *change built-in*, for change is the only constant when it comes to real-world business processes. Oxford professor, Martyn Ould described the task of process architecting, "We work through a rigorous way of defining a process architecture that is aligned solely to the raison d'être of the organisation, and that must form the basis for all thinking about the organisation's processes."[1]

All businesses have an architecture. The real questions are how visible is the architecture, and does it provide for business and technological evolution? Including architectural planning in the business strategy process helps ensure the longevity of business models and information systems through the adaptability inherent in good architecture. Business process management platforms, created under a well-defined work-oriented architecture, exhibit conceptual integrity. This quality helps organize process development projects and lays the foundation for Operational Transformation and technology evolution.

Planning, Strategy and Methods

Adopting new technologies places extensive demands on employees and their managers. Both are expected to change the way they think and work, as individuals and in groups, as automation is extended to new and unfamiliar domains. People must be given time to learn and time to form teams, not just with others in their immediate organization, but with others outside the company. As a company transitions to become a real-time enterprise, treating these realities as constraints is wise.

The lesson is that business process management provides such a strong capability for business change, that organizational constraints and cultural issues surface as the critical success factors. The way out of this dilemma is the *incremental* adoption of business process change that's in step with the propensity for change in the organization. One of the major failings of BPR during the 1990s was that it forgot all about people. Remembering that it is people who make processes work, one of the most essential aspects of executing strategy is a shared understanding of strategic direction and the key factors that will help the firm to win.

But a shared understanding is not enough, for BPM *methods* must rigorously reflect the messy reality of how people actually *do* their work, not the neat and tidy world of computer transaction processing. In his landmark book, *Business Process Management: A Rigorous Approach*, (The British Computer Society, September 2004), Martyn Ould notes, "A lot of process modelling has come from the software engineering world, where, historically, data and information have ruled. That sort of modeling has therefore concentrated on things and data about things. But processes are about dynamics, activity, collaboration and cooperation. So the way we think about processes must have these at the centre. We must put processes back on top."

"At the heart of BPM is a different understanding of business processes. Part of that understanding is that our process is not something that could perhaps be 'deduced' from the way our information system is set up or from what our ERP allows us to do. It is not 'implied' from our information system. Our process has its own separate existence in a form that—given to a process enactment engine [a BPM system]—can be executed or 'run,' that can be changed on the fly, that can be evolved as our business evolves, that can be monitored in real time, and that can be deployed at will through the organisation. A computer system that supports our organisation no longer simply helps us to manage our information: it now helps us, first and foremost, to manage our processes. It is a business process management system. This third wave [of BPM] needs appropriate methods for thinking about processes, for working with processes, for defining, designing and analyzing processes in a way that positions us to use those new BPM systems." The methods Ould describes are centered on real-world processes that are complex, even muddled or messy—as they really are when real people operate real businesses.

What to Think and *Do* Next Monday Morning: Incremental Change

Grand notions of business change are particularly problematic. It all boils down to "what should business leaders do next Monday morning, assuming that's the first day of the ordinary work week in your country. While there are no secret formulas, no cookie-cutter recipes, senior management must recognize the tight link between *business strategies* and the *business processes* that are needed to execute on those strategies. If the leadership of a company has no innovative business strategies it would like to implement, it shouldn't even bother with business process management—no innovative business strategy; no need for BPM; full stop.

On the other hand, creative business strategies that were once thought to be impractical, due to the lack of business process capabilities and the rigid information systems that hindered change, can now be embraced *incrementally* with technology enablement—one strategy, one business process, at a time.

Change, in strategy and change in business processes, becomes a matter of *portfolio management*, not big-bang, disruptive IT investments. Thus, what business executives should do, *next Monday morning*, is to take the first step of making their decision makers BPM savvy—to begin instilling business process thinking throughout the organization. There is much to learn, and cultural barriers to overcome, but Monday morning is a good day to start your company's incremental business revolution, to start your company's step-by-step journey to becoming a process-managed enterprise.

The monolithic enterprise software approach of the past has made the ability to change extremely expensive. But in the real-time enterprise, "agility and expense" no longer tug against one another. Business process management systems provide the flexibility needed for change to be a simple, natural and straightforward proposition. Business process management allows companies to *evolve* their processes without hindrance from their existing, rigid computer applications, significantly reducing the costs of business and technological change. Cost reductions involve both current expense and longer-term *total cost of ownership* of business processes as they, inevitably, change. Business process management systems provide the capabilities for delivering results one business process at a time. Now CEOs can embrace change without cringing at the cost. Investments in new or improved business processes can now be totally incremental propositions.

The effective blending of *people, process* and *technology* is the challenge of transitioning to a process-managed enterprise. With these three critical variables in mind, Figure 11.1 presents the process for transitioning to business process management—and the incremental process of implementing innovative new processes, and improving existing ones.

Value Chain Assessment. The task of value-chain assessment involves the high-level mapping of existing business processes across the value chain, working from the outside-in. The entire process of assessment is driven, first and foremost, by customer buying patterns and behaviors. Major work activities, steps and hand-offs are identified across the entire value chain. The customer is at the center of everything.

Value-chain analysis involves domain experts who define the initiatives to be pursued, based on an analysis of a company's strengths, weaknesses, opportunities and threats (SWOT). Because a company is dealing with an entire value chain, suppliers' and customers' inputs must be included in the SWOT analysis.

Of course, *strategy formulation* is the major outcome of value-chain analysis. Strategy must be tightly linked to business process management capabilities, which are the very capabilities needed to execute on strategy. Strategy formulation creates the vision, frames market opportunity, sets the major goals, defines the metrics needed to measure achievement of the goals, prioritizes the initiatives needed to reach the selected goals, and defines the first-cut organizational infrastructure. Clearly, participation from all the stakeholders in the value chain must be included in the process.

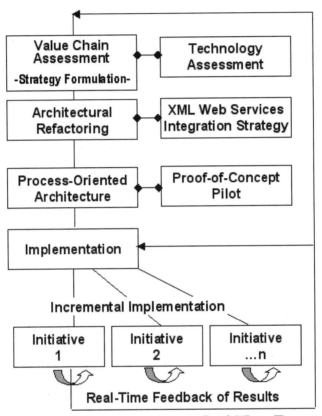

Figure 11.1 Transitioning to a Real-Time Enterprise

Business architecture will greatly impact organizational design within the company and within customer and supplier organizations. All participants must be fully involved, as the lack of willingness to change organizations by any one party can be an insurmountable obstacle. But this does not mean tearing apart organizations with massive change. It is precisely this reason that the transition to business process management must be *incremental,* not the all or nothing, big-bang approach of last decade's internal business reengineering, and the painful installation of huge enterprise application packages.

In parallel with value-chain analysis, technology assessments will reveal existing technical readiness to support business process management—within the enterprise, and the readiness of all trading partners involved. Technology is so vital to business process change that current capabilities must be fully understood if technology gaps are to be closed. Such gap analysis will determine which technologies will be needed to deploy a business process management platform and integrate existing technologies into that platform.

Architectural Refactoring. Because the goal is to build the business process management infrastructure, existing architectures must be analyzed to determine how existing platforms, networks, applications and databases of record can be adapted and integrated into the new framework. In parallel with this architectural refactoring, Web services integration strategies must be developed so that existing information systems, too, can be brought under the umbrella of the business process management system. Architectural refactoring helps determine how existing data-centric technologies and architectures can be integrated into the process-centric platform of the future.

The ultimate process platform will not be built in one big step. The scenario is similar to any large building project, for example, a college campus master plan. The entire campus is laid out providing a total vision of what is to come, but only those buildings that are to initially go up are designed in detail. So it should be with the initial BPM architecture if a hodgepodge is to be avoided.

Initial Process-Oriented Architecture. The results from architectural refactoring provide the initial, first-cut goals, requirements and constraints to be fed into the next step, designing an initial process-oriented architecture. Like a college campus master plan, all components of the new architecture will not be put in place all at once. However, core infrastructure components, such as a business process management system, must be put in place to support initial business process management initiatives.

Proof-of-concept pilot. New business process management projects introduce change in virtually all facets of development—a new development paradigm, new infrastructure, and new roles, skills, responsibilities and organizations. This much change all at once is a sure formula for high risk. Fortunately, risk management can be achieved through proof-of-concept projects that introduce these new facets in a controlled environment.

A proof-of-concept project is planned in the same way as any other project. The differences lie in goal selection, project scope, duration and development pace. The pace for a proof-of-concept project is generally slowed to allow those involved time to learn. Tasks are structured to provide early opportunities for success. It is important that participants build confidence in themselves, and in the architecture and business process design before moving on to more aggressive schedules. New concepts require hands-on experience, and time to be assimilated.

The goal of a proof-of-concept project is to balance risk, and rapidly validate design assumptions. The project must demonstrate value to the organization without introducing unnecessary risk, and allow time for both individual and team learning. With the proof-of-concept project successfully concluded, initial business process management projects can be pursued, signaling the beginning of building the process-managed enterprise.

Implementation. Business process management provides the framework to coordinate and integrate multiple business process automation projects. It provides the capability to discover, design, deploy, execute, interact with, operate, optimize and analyze complex, end-to-end processes. The power of business process management is that it fosters an *incremental* approach that is key to risk management, sustainable growth and reduced cycle times needed to respond to market realities. This incremental approach allows the organization to change priorities and direction when appropriate. This incremental approach also enhances credibility with customers and builds morale among value-chain participants.

Incremental implementation has one extremely important benefit. Huge change initiatives, such as converting to ERP systems, consume huge amounts of time and resources. *Disruption* and *waning support* are the bywords of major, time-consuming change where results from the change are "somewhere in the future." Implementation lessons can be learned from Microsoft and other successful software makers. Once they have "just enough" of a new product, they launch it, producing immediate results and generating a new revenue stream with "Release 1.0." Software product managers know that the complete product is several releases away, but they don't wait for the ultimate product before grabbing competitive advantage from their innovations. They also use the feedback from the early adopters to shape the follow-on releases, thus employing their customers in their product development.

Feedback of results is essential to continuous improvement and the uncovering of fresh opportunities for sustaining the pace of innovation.

Because business process management changes the way a company operates, it calls for commensurate measures of business performance. How else could companies measure their progress in translating vision and strategy into day-to-day business reality? A modern jet airliner requires many more instruments to measure flight-critical performance than an automobile needs for its simpler operating environment. The real-time, process-managed enterprise embraces quality management methods such as Six Sigma to power the digital cockpit instruments managers need to gauge business-critical performance during the journey ahead.

People and Culture: The Critical Success Factors

As said before, BPM isn't an event; it's a way of business. The challenge of becoming a real-time enterprise is to instill business process thinking in all the thinkers, actors and doers in your company—as BPM practitioner, Andrew Spanyi says in his widely acclaimed book, *Business Process Management is a Team Sport: Play It to Win!,* "from the board room to the lunch room."

"In too many organizations, senior management's *functional management* mindset represents one of the most significant barriers to change. Indeed, there is reason to believe that the traditional functional paradigm has done more to impede customer-focused, business performance improvement over the past two decades than almost any other factor. Too often, the driving force for executives is ego. They are more concerned with their authority in their domains as opposed to the flow of value-added activities to satisfy customers and shareholders. Unless this changes, a company's BPM efforts will ultimately fail."

"This way of thinking stands in the way of executives understanding and improving the flow of cross-functional activities that create enduring value for customers and shareholders. It promotes the type of thinking that impedes the effective deployment of enabling information technology. Indeed, one could argue that it's the functional mindset that has been at the core of many rather appalling business decisions in terms of deploying information technologies. It promotes 'silo behavior' and turf protection, and an undue preoccupation with organization structure. Further, it encourages a distorted view of performance measurement and executive rewards, shifting focus away from meaningful measures such as the timeliness and quality of services provided to customers, and toward less significant measures around functional or departmental performance. It reinforces a task focus and traditional command and control behavior instead of empowering cross-organizational teams and their members. Moreover, traditional functional thinking has also led to outdated management practices in the areas of goal setting and problem solving, and it stifles innovation."

Spanyi doesn't just identify problems: "How can you transform the traditional functional mindset such that your organization is designed to make it easy for customers to do business with the company and easier for employees to better serve the company's customers? There is increasing evidence that an effective way of transforming the traditional functional mindset is to embrace enterprise business process thinking by tightly linking business strategy to enterprise business process management (EBPM) practices. What does this involve? Frankly, it requires a lot of very hard work, and concepts which will make some of your executives very, very uncomfortable." In conclusion, people and cultural issues represent the critical success factors for becoming a process-managed real-time enterprise.

Adopting the process-managed way of doing business requires operating discipline. Spanyi elaborates, "When I think of the business practices involved in operating discipline, I'm reminded of a quip attributed to Yogi Berra that says, 'In theory there is no difference between theory and practice. In practice there is!' We've seen that happen over the years with improvement initiatives such as TQM, reengineering, activity-based costing and even with Six Sigma. Enterprise business process management runs the same risk, if we're not careful. In short, much of the work in establishing strategic focus and operating discipline generally takes place at the senior management level. But getting the desired results requires that everyone in the organization be 'on the same page.' That's the essence of operating discipline." That's also the essence of the process-managed real-time enterprise.

References.

---

[1] Ould, Martyn A., "Incremental Process Deployment," January, 2003.
    http://www.cems.uwe.ac.uk/~sjgreen/systemmodellinggroup/Workshop0103/ MartynOuld2.pdf

Appendix A

The Myths and Realities of the Real-Time Enterprise

KEY POINTS: *The Real-Time Enterprise Is Like Teen-age Sex*
  1) It is on everybody's mind all the time.
  2) Everyone is talking about it all the time.
  3) Everyone thinks everyone else is doing it.
  4) Almost no one is really doing it.
  5) The few who are doing it are:
    a) doing it poorly;
    b) sure it will be better next time;
    c) not practicing it safely.

Lately, business writers, IT analysts and software companies are talking about the real-time enterprise, and for good reason. It represents a new way of competing that can revitalize competitive advantage. But with mixed messages coming from software vendors, venture capitalists, management gurus and trade publications, much mystery and confusion surround the term. This book provides a systematic discussion of what a real-time enterprise is and what it portends. Before continuing that discussion, it's helpful to address the myths in order to set the stage for learning what it takes to become a real-time enterprise.

Myth 1. *The crash of 2000 was the end of the business Internet fad.*

The crash of 2000 was actually the *end of the beginning* of the real business Internet. There is no such thing as a *new economy*; there is only the *real economy*. In the real economy, business fundamentals, not pumped-up market caps, count. If the current state of the real economy needs a name, it's the *customer economy* for it's the customer that, with so many choices, has wrested power from producers. Wealth has to be earned the old fashioned way by delivering true value to never-satisfied customers in new and better ways.

With the dot-com clutter cleared away, businesses have come to realize that the Internet has had less that 5% of its ultimate impact on business transformation. That transformation centers on building the real-time enterprise that can sense and respond to changing markets and customer demands, for custom goods and services delivered when and where they want, at a price they are willing to pay.

Myth 2. *The real-time enterprise is just another marketing ploy, more hype.* Besieged by three letter acronyms (TLAs), buzzwords and slogans as the 1990s came to a close, the last thing companies wanted was more hype. But, under the latest TLA hype curve, the RTE, lies substance.

In the past, several industries needed specific real-time operations such as those that could handle airline reservations, automatic teller machines, metered telephone usage and stock market transactions. These companies used fault tolerant computer systems to actually run key aspects of their business operations in real time.

In today's global, instant economy, where competition is but one click away, every business must become a real-time enterprise, stamping out *information lag* in all of its mission-critical operations. The real-time enterprise represents a new way of competing that provides information that is always on and always up-to-date. It provides *actionable information* and the means to act—to conduct business based on that information. Actionable information can be used to speed transactions, synchronize information to reduce float, and provide the feedback companies need to sense and respond to market changes in days or weeks instead of months or years. The real-time enterprise powers its profits with real-time business processes and business process management. The real-time enterprise is a market-driven company that deploys zero-latency business processes spanning people, companies, computers and applications to maximize its performance. It optimizes its entire value chain and implements a sense and respond infrastructure that allows it to adapt to, and proactively shape, ever changing markets.

Myth 3. *In the new way of competing, competition is company versus company.* The good old days of the vertically integrated company, where newspapers owned tree farms to provide paper pulp, and automakers owned many of their sources of raw materials are gone. Today those resources are provided by trading partners scattered around the globe, representing dynamic business webs, where labor and material resources can be optimally provided. Goods and services are delivered to customers not by a single company, but by a complete value chain, averaging more than twenty participants. As a result, today's competition is value chain versus value chain, not company versus company. The optimized value chain delivers the best goods at the best price with the best service to dominate its industry. The real-time enterprise provides the foundation for participants in a value chain to act as one, to become a virtual company, and to manage the total costs of the end-to-end value delivery system. But there is more.

The value chain is a collection of autonomous companies where each company does its work in parallel, according to its own clock, to add value and passes the results along to the other participants in the chain. Today, the term value chain is a misnomer for it's not a linear *chain* at all; it's a synchronized *web* of companies working together to deliver value. In fact, the value chain is not a tangible thing or legal entity, it's an *emergent behavior* that, though no one owns it, harnesses the parallel work of its participants toward the ultimate goal of delivering compelling value to customers. The real-time enterprise takes head on the challenge of asynchronous business processes that span entire, non-linear value webs.

Myth 4. *To win, companies must own their value chains.* Companies don't own their value chains; value chains own companies. But an optimized value chain, where all participants become winners by optimizing the overall system, is no assurance of future success. In fact, when all is going well that's the time companies should worry, for it's markets that ultimately own value chains. Markets cannot be (legally) controlled, and they are full of surprises and shifts.

The real-time enterprise senses change in markets and provides the early warnings needed to adapt to market surprises and shifts. But of even greater importance, the real-time enterprise taps information *external* to its existing value chains to anticipate and shape new market demand—the anticipating enterprise. An optimized value chain is absolutely necessary, but not sufficient in today's market realities. In the words of management luminary, Peter Drucker, "The next information revolution will be on gathering, analyzing and acting on information *outside the firm*, driving a shift in information technology from 'technology' to 'information' as the key focus." In response to changing market threats and opportunities, the real-time enterprise bundles, unbundles and rebundles entire value chains to dominate its industry. Thus while the new way of competing is value chain versus value chain, the marketplace is the ultimate master. To monitor the pulse of the marketplace, companies must complement their value-chain capabilities with far-reaching information chains.

Myth 5. *Prediction-based models are the key to accurately forecasting market demand.* What may appear to be a stable market can be disrupted by acts of God or, more often, by a new competitor that crafts an innovative value chain that disrupts the current status quo—the phenomenon of *creative disruption.* Such change creates shock waves for established value chains because, in order to copy the innovator, companies would have to disintermediate existing channels or radically alter the value propositions and characteristics of its existing goods, services or brands. Such *trade offs* are huge obstacles to agility for established companies. When Dell disrupted the PC industry with its direct sales model, other PC makers could not imitate the model without destroying other parts of their business and existing distribution channels. In a story oft told by management guru, Michael Porter, when Neutrogena introduced a soap that left no film on the body, the Dial Corporation could not match that product characteristic without negating its strong branding for Dial soap that is specifically designed to leave an antibacterial film on the body.

Companies must be strong participants in their existing value chains, but they also must become disrupters that can shift market equilibrium in their favor. It's less useful to predict markets than to shape them with disruptive innovations. Results from early pioneers indicate that the real-time enterprise can measure results better than ever before, and cut business cycle times by 70 to 80 percent, speeding their ability to bring new products or services to market—allowing them to become disrupters. Instead of business as usual—*buy-make-sell* based on market predictions, the real-time enterprise anticipates and even shapes demand, doing business as *unusual, sell-buy-make.* Instead of the philosophy of "build it, and they will come," the real-time enterprise philosophy is *if they come, we'll build it in real time.*

Myth 6. *The company that disrupts an industry with a competitive breakthrough that cannot be easily copied is ensured of enduring success.* The ultimate, end-all company will never happen. By their very nature, markets live on the edge of chaos, characterized by *punctuated equilibrium,* making it difficult for even the disrupter to thrive or survive for long periods. For the long haul, success must be followed by a healthy paranoia because the mathematics of punctuated equilibrium guarantees change. Only the companies that master creative disruption, including their own creative destruction, will be agile enough to adapt to or shape markets. Habits die hard, but the company of the future won't resemble today's. With its central abilities to sense and respond, the real-time enterprise has change "built in," enabling a company to disrupt markets, make course corrections even when it requires its own creative destruction, and adapt again. These fundamentals can enable the real-time enterprise to flourish and sustain competitive advantage.

Myth 7. *The real-time enterprise uses real-time computer programs.* In scientific computer applications such as automated manufacturing applications that drive numerically controlled machines or process-controlled oil refineries, real-time technology is needed. Real time, in this sense, requires real-time computer programs so that the system can control what happens in the external environment in absolute real time. Such programs are typically embedded in the machinery they control.

The real-time enterprise, on the other hand, does not require real-time programming systems, for, in business automation, real-time is typically perceived in a human context. This means that *actionable information* is captured and made available *in-time-enough* to make decisions and act on those decisions. In the worlds of commerce and trade, expensive and exotic technologies used in scientific computing are not needed. What's needed in the real-time enterprise is a way of tapping existing commercial information technologies so that information float can be eliminated. That means an *architectural change* in how existing information systems are exploited to gain a real-time business process advantage.

In short, systems-of-process—where the end-to-end business process becomes the focus of automation—represent an architectural shift in business automation. The idea is to automate and manage the *interactions* of existing function-specific computer applications, also known as *stovepipes* or *islands of automation* (e.g., order entry, inventory, work-in progress and so on), for it is the *interactions* of these discrete systems, not the systems themselves, that make up an end-to-end business process that spans functional business departments and companies in a value chain. The real-time enterprise doesn't attempt to build some monolithic, real-time "killer application," but instead exploits its existing information systems in new ways by automating and managing their interactions as end-to-end business processes. The fundamental shift is that of making the business process a first-class citizen in the world of business automation, and using business process management as the means of managing the *white space* between isolated islands of automation.

Myth 8. *The real-time enterprise is more about technology than organizational change.* Although the real-time enterprise sounds like a marketing slogan to sell speedy new technology, it has less to do with technology than organizational change. The real-time enterprise does require a shift in emphasis on which existing technologies will now play a primary role, but the fundamental impact will be felt most by business people, not technologists. Here's why.

Since the advent of the computer itself, business people have dreamed of "thinking machines" that could automate the entire company and make tactical decisions to enable business change and innovation. Of course, that never happened and computers have, for the past fifty years, been delegated to being digital clerks keeping up with the affairs of the back office. Business computing has centered on after-the-fact record keeping, not the live operations of the business. Today's business systems are so brittle and difficult to change that they are the major obstacles to business change. Executives with innovative ideas know that their visions are often for naught because IT cannot execute on them in time to make a difference. But all that changes in the real-time enterprise. In the real-time enterprise, technology is no longer the obstacle to change, and what early pioneers have learned is that organizational change is now the central challenge to gaining business agility. Such change requires leadership that goes beyond the four walls of a given organization, and requires influencing the behavior of all the companies participating in a given value chain.

Myth 9. *The real-time enterprise is about immediate Web access to a given company's existing information systems.* Purveyors of enterprise application packages have been hard at work Web-ifying their systems. They rightfully claim that customers, employees, suppliers and trading partners can access information to their systems in real time. But that's far from being enough to satisfy the needs of a real-time enterprise because it's not just access to a single company's systems that counts. The real-time enterprise is all about providing information in real time between and among companies that make up end-to-end value chains. It's about live and long-lived business processes that go beyond the domain of any single enterprise package.

The suppliers and trading partners in a value chain have their own information systems and technology platforms—they don't use, nor can they be forced to use, the same enterprise software. The real-time enterprise uses open standards so that end-to-end business processes and the information needed throughout the entire value chain can be shared in a controlled fashion. That doesn't mean exposing all information or private implementations of business processes for any and everyone to see or use. But it does mean sharing actionable information within the context of management controls so that the value chain can be optimized and demand channels can reveal substantive changes in market conditions. Makers of enterprise software packages that extend their architectures to go beyond the functions of their proprietary systems to participate in end-to-end business processes will be the ones that can back up their claims of powering the real-time enterprise.

Myth 10. *The real-time enterprise is a new kind of enterprise application package.* The last decade of business saw a shift from customized, in-house developed information systems to enterprise resource planning (ERP) and other commercial off-the-shelf application packages (COTS). As a result, the first knee-jerk reaction to the term real-time enterprise is, "Here comes yet another application package."

The real-time enterprise is not about another enterprise application package; it's about refactoring existing technology architectures to a business process-oriented architecture (POA) that can drive live business operations, as opposed to after-the-fact record keeping, across the value chain. Instead of being a new application, the new architectural tier supports operations by choreographing the functionality already contained in the many applications deployed by companies. The real-time enterprise is powered by orchestrating systems-of-systems, not by an exotic new enterprise software package. It's about a new overarching structure—an architecture—that rationalizes and connects existing function-specific application components for a higher business purpose. It's not the all or nothing conversion required by the last decade's ERP systems. On the contrary, it's about incremental, step-wise change in response to competitive threats and newly discovered market opportunities where the business process architecture allows for change at the appropriate level without having the "recompile" applications. The real-time enterprise isn't the next "killer app;" it's an architecture for the next "killer company."

Myth 11. *The real-time enterprise is mostly about speed.* The transactional and collaborative aspects of the real-time enterprise do indeed require quick response if operational excellence and business process optimization are to be achieved across the value chain. But there is much more than routine reaction speed at the heart of the real-time enterprise.

The real-time enterprise provides closed-loop feedback so that actions and consequences are made visible in a meaningful timeframe for decision-making. The key to making corrections in mid-course requires access to many sources of information outside the firm and beyond the transactions between value chain partners. The real-time enterprise senses and responds to broader, external sources of information. The real-time enterprise goes well beyond information generated by current and past business transactions and is able to sense and respond to change coming from many sources—sometimes even weather forecasts. The real-time enterprise is far more about sensing and responding than just transactional speed, as a soybean farmer in India can tell you as he taps the Chicago commodity market data over the Web to determine this year's crop plantings.

Furthermore, the real-time enterprise is able to restructure its operations without going through painful and expensive processes such as mergers and acquisitions. For example when Toyota restructured its manufacturing and sales companies into one entity in the 1970s, it took major organizational disruption, time and expense to accomplish the task, as discussed in chapter 2. What Toyota really wanted was to link demand signals directly to manufacturing to eliminate the long cycle times in its sales company. Today this could be accomplished by *virtually* restructuring the companies using systems-of-process.

Myth 12. *The real-time enterprise is about existing business systems ported to the Internet.* Today's information technology is designed for record keeping in the back office. Because the real-time enterprise is about powering the front office (the actual operations of the business, not the record keeping) it must be powered by business processes, not just sharing data contained in today's record keeping systems. But even the data shared between companies and customers must be in a form that's much different from the way data is stored in current function-specific, binary record keeping systems (e.g. the customer database, the inventory database, and so on).

For thousands of years, businesses have used *documents* as the basis for conducting business. But from the beginning of business automation, documents were shredded into bits and held in electronic forms that have little resemblance to the original document. Self-describing XML documents, on the other hand, are digital mirror images of the paper documents with which business people are already totally familiar. No matter how different their computer systems are, companies and their automated systems can all understand the XML documents they use to interact with others. The XML "infobase" brings together data into context to create actionable information that is self-describing, extensible and flexible—and in a natural document format rendered for easy manipulation by systems-of-process and people. This scenario is far different from simply porting existing information systems to the Internet. It's about orchestrating business functions contained in those systems, along with raw data being transformed into meaningful and actionable business documents, for both human and machine consumption.

Appendix B

Cycle-Time Management: A Survey of Six Industries

If You Can't Measure It, You Can't Improve It

In keeping with quality pioneer Edwards Demming's notion that if you can't measure it, you can't improve it, let's examine some of the important metrics associated with creating *value*. From a financial perspective, there are a number of telling ratios that help determine a company's health when compared to the other companies in its sector. These include liquidity, coverage, leverage and operating expense to sales ratios. A simple way to view this analysis is with a spreadsheet that can be generated through data available from a company's income statement and balance sheet, as well as publicly available Service Industry Code data on each market segment. As a cautionary note, these ratios must be reviewed together, not separately, to get the full picture. Plus, from time to time, a company may execute certain business strategies that will greatly affect a ratio from period to period. Any conclusions to be drawn must consider those timeline factors as well.

This model provides a set of benchmarks as to how a given company compares to other companies within its industry and to related industries, if desired. Different industries focus on different metrics to improve their operations going forward. In manufacturing, there is a tendency to focus on throughput, inventory, operating expense, and their associated ratios like Cost of Sales/Inventory, or what is commonly known as inventory turns. The insurance industry focuses on earnings adequacy ratios, capital adequacy ratios, loss ratios and expense ratios. The retail banking industry tends to look at net income to average assets, net income to shareholder equity, net loan and lease losses to average loan and lease finances, risk based capital ratios, tier-1 capital ratios and leverage ratios. Non-profits have yet another set of terms such as unrestricted, temporarily restricted and permanently restricted funds, return on reserves, uncompensated services, liability surplus, and reserves excess. With these overall metrics in mind, let's focus, by industry, on the business opportunities that can be exploited through the enablement of the real-time enterprise.

The Automobile Industry and The 12-Day Car

In the United States, approximately 17 million vehicles are sold each year. The average inventory on the dealers' lots is a two-month supply. By doing the math, that means 2.8 million vehicles are sitting at the dealerships at any given time during the year. At an average selling price of $25,000 this means $70 billion worth of pre-built inventory available for sale. In addition to this inventory, it is estimated that an additional $4 billion in pre-built inventory sits with the suppliers to the automotive companies based on current forecasts.

Given the amount of money involved, much focus has been placed on getting the automotive supply chain to move closer to a make-to-demand environment. Terms like the 3-day car, the 5-day car and the 12-day car are all descriptions of postponement strategies, which exist at various points in the value chain. For example, if an automotive manufacturer is selling a luxury vehicle that has a robust basic configuration with only a few final choices of additional options, then the car maker could keep a pool of vehicles close to an area network of dealerships and offer a 3-day car delivery. If the automotive manufacturer is selling a mid-market vehicle that offers a choice of three option packages without the ability to mix in new options, then they could probably keep a pool of vehicles at a regional level and deliver a 5-day car.

These two scenarios compare favorably to what we have in the U.S. today, which is essentially a 12-day car. Statistics show that in today's market, 80% of vehicles purchased are off the lot after a 1-day dealer preparation cycle. The other 20% are built to order and take as much as 56 days. The weighted average, which is 0.8 times 1 day plus 0.2 times 56 days, is 12 days. The value proposition is very large given that if the auto manufacturer can move to the 3-day or 5-day scenario, it begins to remove huge volumes of stock vehicles, thus lowering inventory and damage costs.

The fantasy scenario would be if the automaker could eliminate all dealership inventory to get to a 100% make-to-order model similar to what Dell has done in the computer industry. For this to happen, automakers need to examine the physical limitations of the supply chain itself. On average in the U.S., backing up from dealer delivery, best practices show that it should only take 8 days to ship a vehicle from an assembly plant to a dealership, 1 day to assemble the vehicle, 1 day to ship parts from the tier 1 supplier to final assembly, and 2 days for the tier-1 suppliers to manufacture and ship the parts—for a total of 12 days. Therefore, if auto manufacturers could modify consumer behavior to be willing to order their vehicles 12 days in advance of delivery, they could theoretically remove the $70 billion plus the $4 billion in parts inventories, for a reduction of

$74 billion. By estimating inventory carrying costs at approximately 10%, this gives the industry a potential savings of $7.4 billion, give or take. While it's not possible to move the entire market to this model, even half is still an impressive savings of $3.7 billion.

Let's examine the automotive problem a little closer. How is a car made? What's the value chain that delivers a new car to a customer? The industry's value chain consists of four basic levels or tiers:

1. The top tier consists of dealers, the retailers for cars and service parts.
2. The next tier includes body and assembly plants and some service parts operations. This tier is usually referred to as the original equipment manufacturer (OEM) level.
3. Below the OEM level are tier-one component suppliers that provide electronic components, transmissions, tires, glass, interiors and so on.
4. Below them, tier-two suppliers include foundries, semiconductor plants, steel mills and the myriad small suppliers of miscellaneous materials and parts.

Historically, the information passed between the participants across the various tiers in the value chain is best described as a "spaghetti flow." In the past, what was available for tier-one suppliers and above had been electronic data interchange (EDI), a cumbersome and expensive technology solution. EDI systems are so expensive and difficult to work with that many tier-two suppliers are excluded from using the technology. Instead, they use manual and unstructured methods of information exchange: mail, fax, telephone and email.

The problem with these EDI transaction sets is that they are very rigid in terms of what, when and how data can be transmitted. This rigidity makes them almost useless for managing the day-to-day activities and operations of the value chain participants. EDI information exchanges are so inflexible and complex that a lot of information that the participants would like to exchange with each other cannot be handled. As a result, what typically happens is that many of the supply chain participants ignore certain EDI transaction sets and end up saying, "Here is what I need for the week, I'll just average it out, take the highs and lows, and I will build protective inventory coverage." That's why $4 billion in inventory is typically carried between the automotive manufacturers and the tier-one suppliers. All they can do is plan production around weekly averages.

In order to improve collaboration between the tiers in the supply chain, auto companies must make significant advances in their electronic communications; otherwise the tier-1 schedules will continue to fluctuate significantly day to day based on a phenomena commonly referred to as the *bullwhip effect*—small changes downstream amplify into huge changes upstream in the supply chain. If upstream participants were to build to what downstream participants said, "I need it on a Monday next week," the next day that information could change. "Well, I didn't really need that Monday, I really need it Tuesday, I need something else on Monday." By using the daily granularity or visibility of EDI transactions sets, it's not clear what the assembly plant would be producing, and it would likely end up losing a lot of money. Given that it is too expensive to change production setups based on changing material requirements by the OEM, the bottom line is that traditional electronic support for managing EDI business transactions do not make the technology very useful for actually running the business.

The challenge is to deploy an electronic infrastructure that is much more valuable in supporting actual business processes and decision making than traditional EDI transaction sets.

Some of the issues involved include:

- Production constraints between the tiers in the supply chain are not visible or well understood.

- Communication lead-time is increased because each tier requires several days to adjust requirements.

- Lower tier suppliers are forced to operate from inflated and fluctuating requirements.

- The parameters driving the scheduling are hidden inside complex systems and are therefore not well understood.

- Systems focus on managing the scheduling process within plants rather than between plants.

From a business process perspective, EDI is a *serial* process. As a result, communication lead-time is increased because each tier requires several days to adjust to new or changed requirements passed through EDI transaction sets. EDI participants do not have the ability to run a *parallel* environment for synchronizing the decision-making among all participants affected by a single transaction. But that's exactly what is needed. Cumbersome serial processes that proceed step-by-step need to be reengineered into parallel processes, so all participants can see relevant information at all levels of the value chain at the same time they make decisions.

Being left out of the EDI loop, lower tier suppliers are forced to operate from inflated and fluctuating demand forecasts. These lower tier suppliers are not able to see changing information fast enough in terms of the decisions that are getting made at higher tiers or in terms of what inventory still sits at the dealership. Questions go unanswered, "Do I have too much of one type of component or are the option take-up rates for power seats not getting picked up fast enough, therefore I shouldn't be making those servo-controls?" Lower tier suppliers simply are not seeing such information. The parameters driving the scheduling are hidden inside complex EDI systems scattered across the top tiers in the value chain, and are, therefore, not well-understood. This is a critical point because it means managers do not get the vital information they need to actually manage the business. Current scheduling systems focus on managing the scheduling process within plants, rather than between plants—plant managers only see what is in their isolated span of control.

To get beyond these issues, technology must be capable of providing support for system-to-system and company-to-company interactions that unlock hidden production constraints and provide information that reaches all the way down to the lowest tiers in the value chain. Right now, the industry just does not have the ability to do that. All it has is EDI with very rigid transaction data sets way up in the top tiers. Because the systems cannot provide the accurate *state* of the entire value chain, participants do not have the ability to manage the end-to-end business process. To be useful, the information systems need to be federated, to act as one.

A more detailed look at these issues reveals that assembly plants have more capacity than the market needs. As a result, they are shut down for certain periods, meaning that value-chain participants must carefully manage what they are building and how they are scheduling their production. And as long as everyone in the supply chain knows that an assembly plant is going to be shut down, they can adjust their schedules and everything remains efficient. That is not what happens, though.

In some automotive companies, it is not uncommon to find that half of the time that an assembly plant is scheduled down for a week, due to reconciliation problems between forecast and demand, the decision to shut down is taken with four weeks or less notice. As a result, no one in the supply chain is able to re-act—they just keep building as if the plant was going to be up and running as usual. Needless to say, that is a big problem. But that's not all.

Hundreds of changes are made to operating plans every single week that the assembly plant is out of production. This can be seen in the EDI transaction sets volatility. Once the plant is back up and running, only seventy percent of the vehicles originally scheduled for a specific week are actually built in that week, and the stability of material releases between weeks two and one is only fifty percent. Because the EDI transaction sets are so volatile, they simply are not used. In lieu of electronic support, phone calls, faxes, and emails start flying. But these forms of communication can create more problems than they solve because they throw everyone in the value chain out of sync. The auto industry needs synchronized information delivered in real time!

The reality remains that the stability of the tier releases between two and one is only 50 percent. Therefore, the lower tier suppliers really cannot build ahead to gain efficiency on their production capacity because of the instability.

Why does it take so long to order a car? By analyzing the order flow, it becomes clear that many entities are involved in moving the materials in the supply chain: dealers, zones that manage the dealers, sales division, the central office, product groups, production control, assembly plants, and allied divisions and suppliers. Activities are actually executed by a particular entity that carries out the functional activity in its horizontal "swim lane."

The current technology approach in the industry coerces supply chain participants to stay in their own swim lanes—a set of systems have been developed to support dealers; another set

of systems have been developed over the years to support
zones, sales divisions, central offices and so on. Every participant does its tasks, but stays in its swim lane. Therein lies the
real problem—white spaces and disconnects between each of
the swim lanes. These disconnects are what causes it to take so
long to make decisions around a vehicle getting ordered, getting
it through all the planning processes, all the processes where
automakers distribute inventory out to the dealerships, and all
the processes to conduct pricing control and assembly. The reason that this works this way is because of the system support
underneath these different groups. They are stratifying the decision-making, making it impossible to run the overall value chain
faster.

What happens if a different approach is taken? Here is what
an experienced supply chain analyst may think, "What if I come
in and take apart that old serial process Vehicle Production
Planning process which is supported by systems that don't talk
to each other, and I put in a different, parallel environment?
What if I can lift the business logic out of the isolated applications and put in a new tier of the architecture to provide a *parallel* vehicle production planning process between the zones, the
sales division, central office, and the product groups, targeting a
one week cycle time?" The same goes for Collaborative Dealer
Planning & Allocation Leveling, and Vehicle Sequencing &
Scheduling. If each of these three major processes can be run in
a single week, we can take an existing 64-day process down to a
21-day process.

Now that the planning cycle has been tightened to 21 days
for the manufacture and assembly of vehicles based on forecasted demand, automakers should be much more accurate,
given that the demand signal is more tightly linked to actual recent purchases by Model/Type/Option/Color off the lot. Plus,

given that the forecast is now planned at day 12 in front of the tier-1 suppliers, the automaker is now able to target a feasible 50% make-to-forecast, 50% build-to-order scenario, narrowing the gap on the potential $3.7 billion in savings.

If participants tap their existing, isolated systems and move and manage crucial data and content across the value chain they can begin to run things in parallel—and they can start to cut down on business process cycle times. Cumbersome serial processes that proceed step-by-step need to be reengineered into parallel processes so that all participants can see relevant information at the same time they make decisions at all levels of the value chain.

The grand notion of the 12-day car is not a solution at the factory or plant level and it's not a solution derived by running the tasks within existing business processes differently. Those same tasks have to be run. It's different in the way the underlying system infrastructure supports inter-enterprise information, so that the entire value chain can actually run in a parallel, instead of a sequential fashion. The shift in platform from isolated systems-of-record to end-to-end business process management makes all this possible. Companies that are able to make these types of changes can deliver the 12-day car to their customers—without the $74 billion inventory burden in the industry!

Insurance

Service-based product industries like insurance, banking and finance have certain advantages over manufacturing in that much of the product is *intangible*—document-oriented and represented in paper or electronic format—with quality of service and business process cycle times being the main focus for improvement. This is in contrast to managing the tangible, physical inventory carried by the consumer goods sectors. Although there are fewer physical product barriers preventing the service-oriented sectors from achieving significant reductions in business cycle times, organizational and business process barriers must be overcome. These barriers to cycle-time reduction center on the process-oriented flows of information that must traverse the organizational hierarchy and require support from multiple legacy systems and third-party information such as credit checks. On the positive side, the new document-oriented standard, eXtensible Markup Language (XML), has matured to the point where many service-based product companies are using the technology to achieve as much as 80% reductions in business process cycle time.

From an insurance industry perspective, new technologies and business models increasingly require insurers to exchange information with external partners such as customers, channels, regulators and exchanges, across the insurance value chain:.

- Independent Financial Advisors
- Service Providers
- Product Providers
- Reinsurers

The insurance industry itself is defined by highly regulated firms that provide financial protection for individuals, commercial businesses, and others against illness, death, loss of property, or losses by a third party for which the insured is liable. Insurance can be divided into three broad categories: Life and Health, Property and Casualty, and Reinsurance.

The functional activities, which occur across the value chain include:

- *Distribution* –providing a real or virtual interface between the consumer and the insurer where sales take place

- *Product Development* –analyzing the market, consumer needs, financial feasibility, and developing insurance products designed to meet consumer needs
- *Policy Administration* –processing of customer information and data and its updating and maintenance
- *Underwriting and Investment Management* –guaranteeing the funds and managing the risks and deployment of those funds in investments that could bring maximum returns at minimum risks and required cash flows
- *Claims Handling and Services* –providing after sales services and account information to a client

To be efficient, insurers need to find ways of effectively integrating their external collaborations with their internal processes, data and systems. Continued merger and acquisition activities have caused many insurers to operate with large inconsistencies in pricing, service and quality. In other cases carriers have attempted to consolidate across other financial services channels, but have yet to achieve significant cross sales due to poor process collaboration.

Tools like data warehousing, online analytical processing and data mining constitute the cornerstone of business intelligence, and have been widely accepted across many industries. Insurance companies, on the other hand, have been relatively slow in adopting these tools, much less building the capacity of a real-time response.

A number of market forces are in play, and they will have a significant impact on the ability to succeed in today's market. Product complexity has kept a certain portion of the market tied to an agent, but interactive Internet technologies are lifting this barrier and allowing the consumer to comparison shop for more complex instruments. Channel conflict between a consumer self-service model and the consumer-agent relationship will be viewed as a threat. Other important forces include industry consolidation, narrowing margins, non-traditional competition and continuous regulatory changes.

In reaction to these market forces, insurance companies are looking to implement changes within their value chains. Distribution channels are shifting away from the front office of insurance companies or their agents. They are instead emerging as portals and Web sites that can distribute information and multiple products focused on a single customer. Strategic alliances and outsourcing the right product from the right supplier will no doubt determine consumer satisfaction.

Product development will be focused on the voice of the customer. Differentiating commodity products from high value-add products will be key. Taking this a step further, the ability to identify business opportunities in potentially large niche markets will be critical. Also, in conjunction with the voice of the customer, managing the entire life cycle of the customer relationship will provide the collaboration required to innovate new products based on predicted consumer demand.

Policy administration is now being enabled by the Internet to provide access to the most recent, accurate and high-quality customer information available. Linking the networks of different companies has made policy-administration work much more efficient and, through newer technologies, provides increased scalability and security at the same time. In total this makes processing and clearing much faster and more efficient. Underwriting and investment management provide the best scenarios to achieve economies of scale and push for the ability to "mass customize" by focusing on customer satisfaction. Customer data can now be made available in ways that greatly increase the leverage across the value chain.

Claims handling and services will evolve as innovative products emerge to address customer needs, supported by new call center technology advancements. Customer self-service can provide a completely new means of feedback that will allow companies to adjust their offerings and increase the adoption and consistent use of electronic channels.

While there are still many internal issues related to specific point applications, legacy systems and disparate information sources, insurers require the ability to analyze their customers' needs in real time and tailor all the business processes in the value chain to effectively meet those needs. The ability to turn volumes of data pertaining to customers, agents, claims and policies into *actionable* information is critical. From an overall value chain perspective, delivering the following capabilities to the business will enhance competitive positioning significantly:

- Insurance agents and brokers can receive automatic prompting of policy renewals to ensure that the coverage is adequate while probing up-sell and cross-sell opportunities.

- Real-time alerts can be used to prompt both channel partners and customers of new value opportunities identified by analytics, broadening the product portfolios of insurers and increasing cross-sell rates.

- Market data can be used to inform policyholders of changes in variable life policy values and investment performance as those changes occur.

- Customers can see their entire portfolio in one spot, in a consistent manner, and can modify and update their portfolios based on their preferences.

- Insurance companies can mine the customer portfolios for cross-sell and up-sell opportunities.

- Claims cycle times can be reduced through the use of workflow enabled business processes.

- Reinsurance companies can take the lead to put together a reinsurance deal with several other re-insurers, each taking a portion of the total risk package.

Competitive shifts in the market are forcing insurers to build out real-time response capabilities. Perhaps the most important of these is the shift from a product to a customer focus. Traditionally, the focus of many insurance IT departments has been on the development and administration of insurance products. As a result, systems tend to be organized around product silos, making a consolidated view of the customer difficult to achieve. It is now clear, however, that the only viable strategy for many insurers is to place a fanatical focus on customer satisfaction and drive their value chain by using real-time customer demand, rather the traditional approach of pushing product into the channel.

Banking and Finance

Financial Institutions are under pressure to manage their top line growth and bottom line costs. Several factors have contributed to this situation:

- *Increasing customer attrition-* The Internet has placed a powerful tool at the customer's disposal that allows for easy comparison shopping in the comfort of your home or office. Competition is but a click away and that often translates into customer attrition.
- *Increasing acquisition costs-* Competition for the banking customer's business has resulted in increasingly generous offers by competitors. Combined with the increasing costs of marketing, collateral and labor, the result translates into increasing costs of customer acquisition.

- *Reduced margins*- Commoditization of banking products by high volume producers and increasing competition creates extreme pricing pressures. Coupled with increasing production and acquisition costs, margins have become razor thin.

Financial Institutions address these problems in different ways:

- Through mergers and acquisitions, financial institutions have increased their revenue base and distributed the fixed costs of the restructured organization on a larger customer base to reduce unit costs.

- Differentiating products from plain vanilla offerings through value-added features, thereby engendering customer loyalty and maintaining price premiums.

- Providing business intelligence that can identify potential attrition among existing customers, identify new customer prospects and support the sales cycle.

Tactical real-time banking applications include:

- Alerts that can be sent to the customers to signal insufficient funds in their accounts, allowing the customers to transfer funds and avoid penalties and or embarrassment.

- Customers who can be notified of interest rate changes so that they can make timely decisions to transfer funds (credit cards), re-finance (mortgages) or move funds to take advantage of higher CD rates.

- Customers who can be informed of maturing CDs to enable them to plan for renewal or redemption in a timely fashion.

- Customer whose requests for payout quotes on mortgages or consumer loans can trigger alerts to account managers so they can determine new needs and pre-empt potential customer attrition.

- Missed loan payments that can trigger alerts that warn management of an increasing risk of default, initiating re-

agement of an increasing risk of default, initiating re-
negotiation of loan terms.

- A change of address, which might indicate a job change
  along with a potential 401K rollover. The event can trigger
  an alert to business development managers, prompting a call
  to such customers to determine any new financial needs.

- Large recurring deposits or large purchases on credit cards
  that can be an indication of high-income customers. Such
  events can trigger alerts to business development managers
  so they can offer wealth management products and services.

- Customer analytics which can identify "next likely to buy"
  products that can serve as cross-selling prompts alerts to the
  customer service agents.

- Changes to market indices such as foreign exchange or interest rates that can be served as alerts to portfolio managers to
  help manage their positions through timely action.

- Customers who can be informed of the changing status of
  their loan applications, which not only reflects better service
  but also reduces telephone calls to the bank and thus the cost
  of service.

The banking industry is more than the high-touch customer
interface the average consumer engages in each week. There is a
significant amount of corporate activity that must also be taken
into account. Let's take a typical example where there is a need
to integrate financial services seamlessly into a set of business
processes. In this scenario the buyer is Utilis Computers, a
computer manufacturer based in the U.S. The seller is Discorp,
a disk drive manufacturer in Hong Kong. The seller's supplier is
a manufacturer that provides platters, components that are assembled into the disk drive. A third party service provider acts
as a shipper, and two banks are involved in the transaction, one

for the buyer and one for the seller. This scenario focuses on the integration challenges typical of multi-party business relationships:

1. In the first set of activities, we run through a business process designed to satisfy an order request.
2. In this second set of activities, we process the order through the systems of the trading partners, as well as their banks and their shippers.
3. In the final set of activities, we ship the product and receive payment.

The ability for the banks to interoperate across multiple nodes within the value chain will determine the overall effectiveness of the value chain itself. Orders and materials cannot be processed without the financial checkpoints being processed as part of the transaction. Whether a company is processing a letter of credit or a receivables transaction, the financial aspects of the process must be integrated. Sellers typically won't reserve production capacity until conditional payment terms have been met. The accounts receivable department has to manually reconcile and input payments data into the ERP system, which can also lead to errors.

There are different levels of integration that can be used at various levels to solve these types of problems:

- *Data integration:* requires an agreement on data representation (syntax and semantics) with legacy techniques like ETL or with the newer approach based on XML schemas.
- *Functional Application integration:* includes an agreement on data semantics plus requires the ability to invoke application functionality through the use of adaptors.
- *Process integration:* includes application integration plus requires the ability to execute a business process flow, invoking appli-

cations for the services at various points in the process. Obviously, it also includes an agreement on data semantics.

An effective Web services strategy will help determine which of these integration approaches best fits the business requirements. While Web services don't provide the integration per se, they do provide a framework to cut across technology platforms using Internet protocols. So while we still need an agreement on semantics, with the ability to invoke application services (adaptors), and the ability to execute business processes (BPM), Web services can facilitate the required inter-operability.

High Technology

In order to take the development of the business case for the real-time enterprise a step further, the targeted financial model must be tied back to the operational performance of the company. For each project proposed in the move toward becoming real time, specific results must be targeted in the appropriate operational measures in order to focus the technology deployments into the areas of highest business impact. The financial objectives such as Market Share, Gross Margins, Revenues and Costs of Labor, Materials and Sales can then be calculated and compared to competitive benchmark ratios. Customer metrics may include Price, Quality, Innovation, and Customer Service Responsiveness performance indicators. In this way we will be able to connect our operational, strategic, market and financial performance together with a balanced and understandable approach.

Using this balanced scorecard model and applying it to the average high-tech company, there are a number of aggressive business metrics that should be targeted for a successful real-time enterprise implementation. These "stretch" targets include increasing revenues 5%, increasing gross margin by 5%, reducing inventory by 30%, flushing backorders 100%, increasing new order volume 4%, improving due date performance 25%, reducing cycle time 50%, and reducing operating costs 10%.

Some of the major segments in high-tech include PCs, Servers, Hard Disks, Storage, Printed Circuit Boards and Semi-conductors. Each segment has its own set of detailed requirements, like the binning, downgrading, and yield management requirements that are somewhat unique to the semiconductor sector. To achieve the targeted business results, we must look deeper into the industry value chain in order to comprehend its complexity from a logistical and process flow standpoint.

It's essentially a four-tier value chain:

- Tier 1. Retail Chains sell directly to end customers. Large retail chains such as CompUSA or Best Buy will blend regional distribution centers, in-store and vendor managed inventories, making the retailer a multi-tier entity in and of itself.

- Tier 2. Product Manufacturers cover many market segments: Industrial Electronics, Consumer Electronics, PCs, Servers, Network Gear, and Software.

- Tier 3. Component Manufacturers provide the Backplane Boards, Storage Systems and other major components that go into the final products assembled by Tier 2 players.

- Tier 4. Semiconductor manufacturers provide the raw material, the silicon wafers and chips that are the heart and soul of all hi-tech products.

A high-tech company's ability to improve demand responsiveness through shorter cycle times is constrained by the underlying architecture of its computer applications. If we examine the typical applications underlying a high-tech business process, we will find time lags, manual intervention, accuracy problems, and functional deficiencies, all of which prevent improved re-

sponsiveness and reduced cycle times. The issues extend into
most of the major business cycles within a high-tech enterprise:

- *New Product Introduction* –High level of engineering change notices, explosion in product variety with fast and shrinking
  product life cycles.
- *Demand Management* –Seasonality of demand for consumer
  and corporate channel products, short and shrinking product
  lead times amidst excess demand for hot products, increasing
  percentage of configured and build-to-order demand, delivery coordination required for complex orders, fast delivery
  time commitments with near perfect accuracy required.
- *Supply Integration* –Chronic part shortages, high percentage of
  cost tied up in part inventory.
- *Operations Planning* –Complex internal and external sourcing
  networks, master scheduling based on complex priorities and
  constraints, customer geography, division and channel allocations require coping with constraints on hot products; complex distribution requirements are easily determined but difficult to fulfill, expensive capacity with long acquisition lead
  time.

Given the need to resolve these issues and constrained by
the rigid design of the underlying application architecture, many
high-tech companies have evolved "ad hoc" business processes
to work around the existing application constraints. The resulting process flows are error prone due to the inability to federate
data or manage information.

Typically, we find a complete mismatch between the underlying application architecture and the desired business processes
required to drive the target results in the real-time enterprise
value proposition. From a technical standpoint, the demand fulfillment process is called a "long-running asynchronous busi-

ness process," which basically means there are multiple groups across the enterprise that need to create, reference, update or delete information independently in order to produce the desired results. To achieve the targeted results, high-tech companies can no longer use existing methods where decisions are tied to a legacy application's batch cycle times or where responses are based on stale information. Instead, they must transform themselves into real-time enterprises so they can quickly respond to changes in information that occur throughout the business ecosystem.

A properly structured make-to-demand business plan addresses each of the contributing factors, targeting economic periods where more focus will be placed on certain measures versus others to drive long-term success. We discussed similar ideas earlier in this book when we talked about Toyota building the capability to switch to variety-based manufacturing techniques in an upturn, and scaling down variety during economic downturns.

Make-to-demand is a broader concept than the traditional high-tech *build-to-order* process. Build-to-order by definition means fulfillment of a single custom order, generally by assembling pre-fabricated parts into various combinations based on information supplied by configuring the desired product features. Going forward, build-to-order will be just the fulfillment component of the more strategic vision of make-to-demand, where companies use *marketing and innovation* to shape demand. This approach is directly in line with principles articulated by management luminary, Peter Drucker, "Because its purpose is to create a customer, the business enterprise has two—and only two—basic functions: marketing and innovation. Marketing and innovation produce results: all the rest are costs."

The high-tech process improvements enabled by implementing a real-time enterprise infrastructure include:

New Product Introduction —Tight linkage between R&D and Production, engineering changes based upon "use up" algorithms to decrease rework and parts cost; utilize demand forecast to drive up inventories for new product introduction demand spikes only; end of life planning seamlessly translates old part numbers into new part numbers for planning purposes; plan optimal product cutover dates based on customer service level modeling and inventory obsolescence modeling

Demand Management — Allocate demand to the optimal plant, based upon business objective functions such as: maximize customer service, minimize work in process, maximize capacity utilization, maximize profit; slot demand into the supply pipeline based on demand priorities and netting; re-slot based on changing priorities; plan demand, material supply, and capacity simultaneously, rather than serially; time production to end just in advance of customer demand; allocate the most scarce supply among customer channels; treat upstream ship supplier and downstream customers as part of a virtual supply chain.

Supply Integration — Synchronize all material procurement with availability of scarce chips from upstream suppliers and availability of resources in production; establish supplier flexibility fences and forecast to drive procurement, but produce based on actual customer demands; kanbans for cheaper, readily available components

Operations Planning and Scheduling — Synchronize flow of material from station to station to increase touch time percentage; dynamically substitute parts without generating manufacturing orders for primary parts; coordinate assembly of multi-line orders so that each line is completed simultaneously; intelligently split lots across pooled work centers; utilize work cells with pooled equipment resources; use less rigid line configurations;

schedule setups to meet customer demands while minimizing non-available machine time; reschedule backlog whenever order mixes, volumes, due dates, or supply capabilities change; real-time "available to promise" based on actual resource availability rather than standard lead time or forecast consumption; real-time scheduling of customer orders; build and configure to order; distribution planning linked tightly with production planning; flexible pegging of work in process to demand; separate ordering and scheduling of components from ordering and scheduling of packages; shipping capacity considered at order promising time; returns immediately visible within the supply pipeline for reuse.

While the cultural and organizational issues implementing these types of business process changes are significant, the technology is no longer the challenge it once was when companies like Cisco, Dell, Sabre, and Federal Express developed proprietary systems to enable the types of process changes required to create the real-time enterprise. Given the increased flexibility we now possess, let's now look at the application component functionality we would like to bring into our new business processes in order to achieve the business metric targets in the value proposition.

New Product Introduction – Analysis to determine plan and schedule impacts of different ECN cutover dates; part date effectivity within a Bill of Material; part use up and switch over logic; instant propagation of order mix; demand variability immediately reflected in procurement plans; impact of demand variability on capacity automatically modeled.

Demand Management – Detailed planning horizon encompassing multiple periods; seasonality modeled into demand; automatically adjust inventory build ahead with desired customer service levels based on predicted demand; expedite material on demand; model and execute short term response to market fluctuations; profit optimization; ability to peg components to orders; ability to generate lot size of one; maintain connection between components going to the same assembly; order date quotes based on current system constraints around capacity, finished goods, unassigned work in process; unassigned parts, scheduled receipts, supplier capacities and transportation; time phased yield planning.

Supply Integration – Substitute and alternate parts functionality; supplier capacities or allocations modeled into our process; customer allocation capabilities; business impact analysis for competing demand fulfillment scenarios; consolidation of part orders within user defined time windows; intelligent sourcing based on supplier capacities, costs, and lead times; optimize choice of supplier based on manufacturing and stock locations;

Operation Planning and Scheduling – Include multiple nodes in the manufacturing/distribution network within the business process; model capacity agreements with suppliers; generate work in process pull orders from node to node; factor transportation time from node to node; implement business rules for alternate routings; protect certified routings; manufacture subassemblies to a product family level forecasted demand order; order fulfillment sequencing options, external data feeds to determine order priority; algorithmic based order sequencing; interactive adjustment of allocation levels; material or capacity allocation; hierarchical allocation spanning geographies, customer segments, channels, customers, or user defined identifiers; factor upstream capacity and material constraints in the distribution plan; simultaneous consideration of capacity, material, distribution, transportation, and demand.

However, we are not done building our business case for the real-time enterprise. Thus far, we have analyzed our financials, competitive position, operational metrics, cycle times, application architecture, business process workflows, and targeted component functionality. We must now examine the detailed cost buildup within the workflows themselves to prove whether the planned component functionality will in fact achieve the desired business results. We must map our new processes and functions against this model to calculate the ROI associated with implementing the real-time enterprise. The approach is to break down the value chain into its detailed nodes in order to better match the application component functionality to the point where the value will be realized. This approach has not been feasible in the past, given the rigid packaged applications available in the market. However recent and proven technical innovations have given us the ability to assemble specific component-based application functionality to support more efficient business process designs.

As in most deployment planning, the devil is in the details. If the business and technical gatekeepers can agree on the combination of organization, process and technology changes that will result in hitting the targeted improvements in both these types of cost figures, as well as targeted revenue figures consistent with the overall goals for the real-time enterprise, then success is at hand.

What we can readily see from this example is that the significant improvement potential for the average high-tech company will largely go untapped due to a rigid application architecture that has not been designed to meet the needs of a constantly changing market environment. On the other hand, if a more flexible application architecture can be deployed, coupled with a standard method to model business processes and information flow, then the resulting competitive advantage could be tremendous.

Apparel

The value chain structure for the apparel industry requires complete integration between the textile, apparel, and retailer companies due to seasonality impacts and the related rapid pace of new product introduction. It's essentially a six-tier value chain:

- Tier 1. Retailers
- Tier 2. Distribution Centers
- Tier 3. Apparel Companies (domestic and off-shore cutting, sewing and fabrication of the product)
- Tier 4. Fabric Companies (knitting, weaving, dyeing, cutting)
- Tier 5. Spinners (yarn spinning)
- Tier 6. Fiber Suppliers

In addition to the steps outlined in the real-time enterprise analysis for High Tech, it is instructive to also look at the value-chain business drivers for each node in the value chain. The issue in the apparel industry is that the various nodes in the value chain strive to maximize their own operations, rather than those of the other nodes within the chain. In the high-tech example, we discussed that culture, organization, business process and technology issues must be addressed as a group in order to achieve the real-time enterprise. However, at the value-chain level, it is difficult, if not impossible, to control these aspects of a company's trading partners. By focusing on the drivers, we can come to an agreement as to how to maximize our own drivers, as well as those of our trading partners. We can enable this level of cooperation by applying collaborative technologies that are available today. It is critical that any collaboration which takes place between these nodes be flexible enough to accommodate changing business process needs and requirements, as well as to automate a collaborative process designed to deliver new products at least four times each year, which is the baseline for the apparel industry. The technology architecture of the real-time enterprise provides an environment designed to make this level of collaboration a business reality.

The complexity in the apparel industry lies in the nature of its demand. To understand the demand, we must take the monthly style/color forecast, and net out the orders; break it into the distribution centers from where products will ship; the distribution center forecast must be split into weeks based on historical ratios; the stock keeping units or SKU's must be calculated by estimating size percentage breakdowns by geography; the safety stock must be calculated at the Distribution Center/SKU level to ensure serviceability. Factors like the peak activity associated with the back to school rush must be planned early due to the inability to add additional capacity quickly. Thus, cycle time becomes critical due to the need not to commit to a certain set of styles or fashions until the last possible moment.

Let's look in more detail at the apparel company since they own the brand and, in most cases, carry the hammer in the overall value chain. If we analyze the lead time for the fashion line, we find that it can take as long as 18 months for a complete cycle, with Design/Budgeting/Merchandising being 6 months, Sourcing taking 5 months, Sales/Assortment Planning taking 3 months and Customer Service/Deployment taking 4 months. That means, for instance, that if you were planning the Spring 2005 season, which targets to have all inventory available at the warehouse by December 2004 due to concept ship requirements, then you would need to start the Design process in July 2003 and make the Sourcing commitments by May 2004. This means the company is being forced to commit to a fashion and design gamble before they even get the results from the Spring 2004 selling season. It is critical that this 18 month cycle time be reduced to a 15-month cycle by reducing the final 7 months into 4 months and thereby gaining the ability to consider the full results from the Spring 2004 season before making the final sourcing commitment for the Spring 2005 season. It has been proven multiple times over the past few years that the technology is now available to reduce process cycle times by 80% or more; however, the larger challenge may still lie in the process change requirements.

The target for the real-time enterprise is to provide an infrastructure that can both deliver the desired process flows by assembling a specific set of standards-based application components, as well as extend the appropriate existing legacy systems as part of the solution. Typical targets by major business process for the apparel industry include:

- *Design, Budgeting, and Merchandising* –Automatic allocation of budgets; sales and merchandising scorecards, rules, policies, and business processes fully integrated;

- *Sourcing* –Integrated budgeting and sales planning process at the unit plan level with merchandising projections; sourcing analytics; dynamic sourcing; supplier capacity and material planning visibility; trim optimization;

- *Sales and Assortment Planning* –Automate assortment planning process with buyer business processes; integration of assortment planning, budgeting, sales, and merchandising; confirmation of orders at line opening; style/color/size attribute based planning and allocation.

- *Customer and Service Deployment* –Analyze impact of reorders in real time; increase visibility into shipments and receivables; provide interactive distribution planning.

Consumer Packaged Goods

Cost has traditionally been the all-consuming focus for the typical CPG company. Retailers like Wal-Mart have continued to push the envelope in terms of price reductions, which, in turn, has driven CPG companies to focus heavily on cost in order to turn a profit and participate as a supplier to major retailers like Wal-Mart. However, there are a number of other targets, which tend to garner as much or more attention as cost in today's consumer-focused economy. This includes, of course, not only market share but a host of other targets including perfect order fulfillment, zero stock-outs, margin per square foot of shelf space, revenue per square foot of shelf space, promotional performance, case order fill rates towards 100% from an average of 80%, high rates of repeat business, and synchronization of promotion and pricing lift.

Using the brewing industry as an example, Figure A.1 reveals a mature value chain where much of the costs associated with each node in the chain has been squeezed out over the years. It is critical to never have a stock-out at retail, and the only way to gain true advantage is through volume and market share. High performance information flows and collaborative business process capabilities between the nodes in the value chain are critical to capitalize on the sales opportunity.

Looking across to the potato chip segment, we find a similar situation where the goods move from farms to trucks to processing plants to truck to distribution centers to stores to consumers. Both CPG sectors are mature and, through the years, every penny of cost has been squeezed out of the chain.

In looking at these two CPG sectors, we can also find new ways to increase revenues, such as the opportunity to exploit cross-category pull. Can we increase sales of potato chips by placing a promotional offering on a wing display or an end cap close to the beer section? Can we track that information and either increase or decrease volumes based on the effectiveness of the promotion, the cross-category pull, or both? This scenario is a challenge for the real-time enterprise architecture.

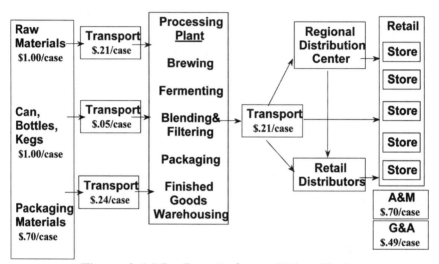

Figure A.1 The Beer Industry Value Chain

Cross docking is also popular across CPG categories. Rather than have less than full truck loads dropping the same product at multiple locations, why not have all those trucks meet at a distribution center and load a new set of trucks that can deliver a full order of multiple items to an end customer? If managed properly, this can be a big win for all parties involved, especially the end consumer in terms of decreased costs.

In general, it is the overall opportunity around improving demand fulfillment that seems to get companies most excited in this sector. This challenging opportunity manifests itself in the following ways: demanding consumers and retail business partners; category management performance at the store shelf; high expectations for order fulfillment; pressure to take costs out with innovative technology; squeeze on profit margins from store brands and generics; data on market intelligence complicated by many relationships to track; forecasting based on seasonal and promotion lumpy history; excess inventory to compensate for lack of partner coordination; fill-rate performance expectations; customer forward buying based on deals; product substitution and market share dominance; product proliferation; SKU explosions; cannibalization of brand allegiance; and increasing marketing activity and promotions.

Increasingly, the issue in CPG isn't just about serving demand, but it is also about the ability to *scale* and *extend* the business architecture faster than anyone else in the market in a cost efficient manner. For example, beer sales have been increasing on average for the past 10 years. If we look at how the business architecture must be planned to support that expansion, we can sum the issues in Figure A.2. If the technical architecture for the real-time enterprise isn't designed for rapid business expansion and flexibility, in addition to providing the advanced capabilities around sensing and responding to market demand, then only half the problem will have been solved. The key to implementing the real-time enterprise is to enable the business to not only solve the short-term tactical issues related to proactive demand management, but to also provide a low cost, standards-based, easy to maintain technical architecture that can enable core shifts in business architecture, immediately hitting those market windows as they open. It has been proven in numerous studies that the first company to hit a market window typically takes the lion's share of the available profits.

In order to effectively plan out a strategic architecture, we must analyze the *types* of CPG supply chains we would be moving into real time. There are three basic business architectures:

- *Warehouse oriented* –those who deliver from their warehouse to a customer's warehouse that delivers directly to a retail store.
- *Wholesale/Distributor oriented* –those who deliver from their warehouse to a wholesaler's warehouse. Jobbers deliver to individual retail stores.
- *Direct Store Delivery (DSD) oriented* –those who deliver from a warehouse directly to a retail store.

Companies in the Entrprise	Current	Projected	
Companies in the Entrprise	3	10	Future Purchases
Production Facilities	12	20	Future Purchases
Customers	2,000	20,000	Direct to Retail
Ship Points	2,400	24,000	Direct to Retail
Products	1,600	3,200	Increases in brands, pkgs, containers, pallet configs
Production Facilities/ Ship Points/Products	240,000	500,000	
Distributor Fcast	840,000	160,0000	SKU/distributor/month
Transport Routes	4,200	120,000	

Figure A.2 Value-Chain Architecture and Projected Volumes

In reality, many of the larger CPG companies actually run all three of these architectures in different parts of their business. The challenge is to make sure companies don't assume the real-time enterprise is a one size fits all. The real upside with the real-time enterprise is that the technical architecture is designed to deploy a set of infrastructure standards, while still leaving the flexibility to support the specific needs of the various value-chain architectures deployed in the CPG company.

Index

About the Authors

You can reach the authors by email:
rte@mkpress.com

PETER FINGAR, Executive Partner in the digital strategy firm, the Greystone Group, is one of the industry's noted experts on business process management, and a practitioner with over thirty years of hands-on experience at the intersection of business and technology. Equally comfortable in the boardroom, the computer room or the classroom, Peter has taught graduate and undergraduate computing studies in the U.S. and abroad. He has held management, technical and advisory positions with GTE Data Services, American Software and Computer Services, Saudi Aramco, EC Cubed, the Technical Resource Connection division of Perot Systems and IBM Global Services. He developed technology transition plans for clients served by these companies, including GE, American Express, MasterCard and American Airlines-Sabre. In addition to numerous articles and professional papers, he is an author of six best-selling books. He brings that knowledge to life in his provocative talks that deliver business insight and actionable information for executives determined to dominate their industries. Peter has delivered keynote talks and papers to professional conferences in the USA, Austria, Canada, South Africa, Japan, United Arab Emirates, Saudi Arabia, Egypt, Bahrain, Germany, UK, Italy and France.

JOSEPH BELLINI is the Senior Vice President of the Software Products and Services Division at Brooks Automation, a global leader in the semiconductor manufacturing industry. Prior to joining Brooks, Mr. Bellini was CEO of the publicly traded software company, eXcelon, which was acquired by Progress Software in 2002. Prior to eXcelon, Joe was CEO of C-bridge Internet Solutions, an MIT-based startup company. Joe took C-bridge public in 1999, and C-bridge grew rapidly, being ranked as the second fastest growing company in New England. His 20 years of software-related work experience has embraced engineering, marketing, sales and executive management at companies that include i2 Technologies, Oracle, EDS and GE. Mr. Bellini also sits on the board of Yantra, a distributed fulfillment applications provider. Joe holds two Bachelor of Science degrees from the University of Massachusetts in Applied Mathematics and Statistics and Mechanical Engineering. He is also an alumnus of Harvard Business School and holds a U.S. Patent for Extended Supply Chain Planning.

Watch for forthcoming titles.

Meghan-Kiffer Press
Tampa, Florida, USA
www.mkpress.com
Advanced Business-Technology Books for Competitive Advantage